S0-BNC-278

Unless Recalled Earlier
DATE DUE

DEMCO, INC. 38-2931

STREET

TENTH

Mary + House

Ms. B
Apartment

M ST

the Tom's
Laundromat

"1118"
The Old
Clinic

STREET

Giant
Food

dresser

STREET

Veneta Masson

Ninth Street Notebook

Voice of a Nurse in the City

Please address all inquiries to:
Sage Femme Press
PO Box 32124
Washington DC 20007
202.338.9623
sagefemme@starpower.net

Cover sketch by James L. Hall

Design by Lisa M. Carey

To the people of Community Medical Care:

Everything is held together with stories....

That is all that is holding us together,

stories and compassion.

"Winter Count 1973"
Barry Holstun Lopez

CONTENTS

Me, in the mid-1970s, sitting on a pyramid outside
Cairo. Little did I know how dramatically my life
was about to change.

This book tells two stories.

The first is the story of my years as a nurse in a small inner-city clinic, the people I worked with, and some of the people I took care of. The second is a story of the nursing profession as I lived it and reflected upon it from my post at the ragged edge of a massive, dysfunctional health care system, both famous for the medical miracles it has spawned and infamous for the conflicting sets of social and economic values that have shaped and encumbered it.

I tell neither of these stories as a simple narrative, flowing smoothly from beginning to end. What I offer is more like an album — a collection of articles, notes, and memorabilia that, taken together, offer the sense of a whole. It is organized around a series of essays I wrote for various nursing journals — think pieces with their origin in anecdote, representing my attempt to get at the stuff of nursing and health care. To flesh out the essays and provide a context for them, I've included a few of my poems, excerpts from the clinic's annual reports written by me or my colleagues (who offer their own perspective on some of the issues I address) and a couple of entries from my journal, one from 1980 and the other from 1995, to mark the span of years the book encompasses.

You should feel free to browse around in this book just as you would in an album. While the writings are ordered and captioned to provide a sense of continuity, they are not strictly chronological. You will find some repetition, especially in descriptions of the clinic, its staff and my professional history. This is because, when I first published them, I did not assume that readers of any given essay would have read or remembered previous ones. I am extending you the same courtesy.

And now,
    in the tradition of storytellers, I begin.

Once upon a time, in the year I turned thirty, I was transferred to
Washington, DC, to fill the position of Director of Nursing for Project
HOPE, an international health organization I had worked for in Texas
and Brazil. Because my job required extensive travel, I found it difficult
to get established in my new hometown. But I did find a church.
In that church one Sunday morning, I happened to hear a man about
my age, a physician, invite participation on a task force to create a
health ministry in one of Washington's needy neighborhoods. Ah! I
thought. A way to connect with the community. A way to feel like a nurse.

The man was Jim Hall. And the health ministry that we founded
two and a half years later with the blessing and support of the Church
of the Saviour was Community Medical Care, a clinic offering office
and home care to children, adults, and seniors in a rough-and-tumble
neighborhood of inner-city Washington called Shaw. Jim had been
a research pathologist bound for academia. I had mapped out a career
in international health. But in committing to the mission of CMC,
Jim and I embarked on a journey of faith and discovery from which
there would be no turning back.

When we began I was a nurse out of practice, wondering what
I was supposed to do in this primary health care setting. How would my
role and Jim's complement each other — or would they? How could
we work together as nurse and doctor to meet our patients' needs?
By the time I added the chores of clinic director to my nursing duties a
few years later, the country had entered a new era of health care reform
or, more aptly, upheaval. I faced a host of managerial, political and
financial challenges related to third-party reimbursement for medical
and nursing services, government regulation of health care facilities, and
the uneasy interface between hospital and community care, to name a few.

I also wondered about my profession. What does it mean to be a good nurse? What is the art of nursing? Can the healing art flourish in a culture wedded to speed, technology, and the bottom line? Where do I as a nurse fit into what we euphemistically call the health care system?

All of us try to make sense of the things that happen to us. I do it by writing. Spilling the remains of a day into a journal had become a habit of mine even before my odyssey with Community Medical Care began. I had also been producing a steady stream of publications based on my work in international health. As I shifted focus from Project HOPE to CMC, it didn't take long before I found myself sifting through a whole new batch of experiences and putting them into words.

One day, while attending a nursing conference, I joined a roundtable discussion on the journal *Nursing Outlook* led by Lucie Kelly, its editor. When she asked us what regular features we would like to see, one person suggested a column on international nursing. Yes, I thought, I'd like that. I could even write it. But I knew I wouldn't. My head, heart, and hands were engaged elsewhere — in and around the little clinic in what locals sometimes call "the other Washington," not the nation's capital, but the place many of the half-million people who live here call their hometown.

Next morning, while getting dressed for work, I had a brainstorm. I was writing anyway. Why not offer to do a regular feature for *Nursing Outlook*? I knew many of *Outlook's* readers held positions of responsibility away from the fray of hands-on nursing. Wouldn't they enjoy reading an occasional dispatch from the front lines? I could use my clinic as a vantage point from which to look at the larger world of health care and to address themes related to health care administration and financing, the role of the nurse in primary health care, clinic and home-based health services, and so on. After reading a few sample manu-scripts, Lucie decided to take a chance. The column was born. I told her I wanted to call it "Microcosmos" after the collection of short piano pieces by Bartok that I happened to be working on, and because it occurred to me that I was always describing Community Medical Care as a microcosm.

Not all of the essays in this book first appeared in "Microcosmos." I subsequently wrote columns for the *American Journal of Nursing* ("Progress Notes"), and for *Nursing and Health Care Perspectives* ("Art in Practice"). "Nurses and Doctors as Healers," which explains how I came to conceive of nursing and medicine as opposite but complementary poles on a healing continuum, appeared in *Nursing Outlook* before I started writing the columns. An essay on HMOs for Medicaid recipients was published by the *Journal of Christian Nursing*.

During the years I wrote the columns, our clinic moved twice: from Ninth & L to Ninth & P when we lost our lease, and (yes!) back again eight years later. You'll hear about the move and get acquainted with the staff, especially Jim, Sharon, our big-hearted and streetwise patient care coordinator, and Teresa, who first came to CMC as a graduate student in nursing from Catholic University. Katrina, Edy, and then Dorothy held the position of medical assistant (or health aide, the term we used in the early years) between 1980 and 1995. In 1991, Jessica was hired as a receptionist. And, at different times, we had a counselor, development coordinator, outreach worker, and a maternity program in affiliation with the nurse-midwifery faculty practice at Georgetown University. Although the composition of the staff changed slightly over the years, it was always small, stable, and dedicated to the work at hand.

In retrospect, I realize that I was on a quest during my years at Community Medical Care. Among the things I was searching for was a deeper understanding of professional nursing and the work of caregiving today. I believe that through my practice, both clinical and literary, I found it. Whether you as reader will be satisfied with the conclusions I have drawn, I don't know. But I want to tell you that, in putting together this book, I was thinking of you.

If you are a nurse, I hope this book will offer you another perspective on our profession and grist for the mill of your own experience. If you are a nursing student, I hope you will be interested in how, through my practice, I came to see nursing as part of what I call a healing continuum, and in how I responded to some of the challenges I faced in the real world of health care. If you are a teacher, I would like to think you could use one or more of these short pieces to introduce health care topics or to spark a lively discussion. And for those of you who are not nurses but care about health professionals who are trying against the odds to practice the healing art with skill and compassion, bless you. May this book help you to put a human face on nursing and health care at the turn of the 21st century.

A birthday party in the waiting room at Community Medical Care

You will find some version of this mission statement inside the front cover of each of Community Medical Care's annual reports. In the sparest of terms, it tells who we are.

Crossroad Health Ministry, Inc. is a nonprofit, tax-exempt corporation formed by a group of people within the Church of the Saviour to provide health care and the ministry of healing within impoverished neighborhoods of Washington, DC.

In September 1978, Crossroad Health Ministry opened a family practice center called Community Medical Care on the first floor of a renovated townhouse on Ninth Street, Northwest. CMC's mission today is the same as it was then: to receive each person who comes in the wholeness of body, mind, and spirit; to offer comprehensive, high quality, personalized medical and nursing care; and to create an environment in which healing of the whole person can take place. We are also called to care for the sick and isolated elderly of the neighborhood in their homes.

Community Medical Care
at Ninth & L

An excerpt from my journal on January 2, 1980. This is the year I began my chronicle of life at the clinic. Katrina was CMC's first health aide. Although Sharon was originally hired as receptionist and office assistant, this limited role soon evolved into a considerably broader one: patient care coordinator.

Wednesdays are relatively quiet at Community Medical Care until evening office hours begin at 5 PM. Between phone calls, Katrina and I chat about our holiday celebrations and prepare with moderate enthusiasm to distribute some fliers describing our home care program in the neighborhood. It feels good, walking up Ninth Street along the frayed ribbon of townhouses, small businesses, and shops, dilapidated or boarded up, awaiting the inexorable wave of renovation. It is bright, crisp, and clear — and we are at home, accepted if not always known to residents, shopkeepers, and the club at what we call the "wino bench" a couple of doors down from the office.

We tune in to the low hum of activity, barely perceptible to casual passers-by.

Drug dealers and down-and-outs warm their hands over the fire barrel in a vacant lot.

An occasional middle-class homesteader, small child in tow, hurries up to the new Giant supermarket four blocks away.

Art, the burly, black printer smiles and waves an inky hand from the window of his shop, crammed with ancient machinery and piles of smudged paper.

The old German standing in the doorway of his electrical supply store makes a polite half-bow, then retreats behind the iron grates which afford him tenuous security from break-ins.

There's Benjo's on the corner, where Katrina and Sharon cash their paychecks and buy Cokes and peanuts, and where the winos buy their booze and carry it back to the bench in small plastic cups.

And the industry of the Chinese laundry next door to our office where the Toms and members of their extended family watch over the coin machines in which most of the neighborhood people do their laundry and where a number of them first hear about Community Medical Care.

The empty block across the street, razed to make room for a new campus of the University of the District of Columbia, will not be built after all unless Mayor Barry can work his will with the District Committee in Congress.

Ninth Street, urban wilderness, home of the brave, if not the free.

PHOTO: JIM HALL

Ninth Street near CMC

Working in partnership with Jim Hall, physician and founder of Community Medical Care, gave me an invaluable opportunity to observe how nurses and doctors use their expertise in problem solving and nurturing to heal. This essay, published after we had worked together for seven years, was my attempt to express what I had learned.

"With all those degrees and being as smart as you are, why didn't you just go on and become a doctor?" An arresting question for a nurse these days. It was put to me by Mac, a friend and patient, back when Community Medical Care, our family medical practice, had just organized as a small nonprofit corporation offering office and home care. Patiently, I explained that it was not a question of "going on," that nursing and medicine were two different professions and that, of the two, I had chosen nursing. "Didn't you ever want to be a doctor?" Mac persisted. "Not really," I said, for this was almost true.

Yet Mac's questions to me were in fact my questions to myself during the first years at CMC. How is nursing different from medicine and why did I choose the one over the other? Our patients' perceptions of me and my role usually proved less than illuminating. There was Mrs. Casey. After two appointments during which I taught her a diabetic diet, clipped her toenails, and did a routine pelvic exam (like many of our female patients, she is more comfortable with a female examiner), she pronounced: "You're one of those nurses who does just about everything the doctor does, aren't you? Don't they call that being a medical nurse?"

Then there was Mr. Taylor, a retired master chef whom I regularly visited at home to monitor his diabetes and hypertension. Leaving our office one afternoon after an appointment with Jim, he said to me confidentially, "I told Dr. Hall it's always nice to see his nurse. Yeah, but just like they used to say to me when they came into my kitchen, 'We need the helpers, but the chef is best!' "

Pete Merton used to greet me along Ninth Street with a hearty "Hey, here comes the prescription nurse," presumably because I occasionally wrote prescriptions for him over Jim's signature. For a woman who has been to our office once or twice, there is a flash of recognition in an apartment house elevator, "Oh, you're the nurse up to Dr. Hall's," Dr. Hall's being preferred by our patients over Community Medical Care as a name for the practice.

When I am at Mae June Wilson's assessing the status of various chronic diseases and supporting her weight loss regimen, she introduces me to a visitor as "my nurse." On the other hand, while I am fitting Julie Meyers for a diaphragm in our office, she asks if I will be her "personal doctor." Crusty old Mr. Hammersmith was perfectly clear about what he wanted on my first visit to his apartment. "I don't need a doctor," he said. "I need a nurse. You are going to be my doctor *and* my nurse. You're going to do all of it!"

Like me, the nursing profession has wrestled with the question of what nursing is. And like me and CMC's patients, the profession realizes that nursing and medicine are inextricably intertwined. In the literature, one reads of the care-cure philosophy of the healing professions according to which nurses care and doctors cure. But how can the two be separated, I ask myself? And when does care become cure? Some nurses have sought to appropriate for nursing the area of health promotion and disease prevention, leaving to medicine the realm of illness and its treatment. But it is impossible to draw a line marking the border between health and illness. Is an otherwise healthy woman with a minor vaginitis discovered in the course of a routine examination sick or well? What about the person coping successfully with chronic disease? the child with a cold? Should the nursing profession adopt the view that health and not illness is its primary concern, there would also be the embarrassing fact that 70 percent of nurses work in hospitals full of sick people interested in getting well. Likewise, most nurses in extended care facilities and in the community are engaged in helping the sick to get better.

In 1980, the American Nurses' Association boldly declared that nursing is the diagnosis and treatment of human responses to actual or potential health problems.[1] I use the adjective "bold" because it used to be said by and of nurses that they do many of the same things a physician does except that they do not diagnose or prescribe treatment. Here we have those two acts placed right at the heart of nursing. In its original statement, the ANA Congress for Nursing Practice added that nurses diagnose and treat only responses to health problems, not the problems themselves, but practicing nurses mounted a protest, claiming that such a distinction cannot be made. The qualification was deleted in subsequent editions of the statement.

As for me, I began to conduct a self-study. In 1980, I even kept a journal of life and work at CMC. In particular, I observed myself in relation to Jim. I noticed how Sharon, our patient care coordinator, decided which of us a given patient should see. When we worked together with a patient, I noted which questions patients asked me rather than Jim and what they wanted to hear from him, whether or not I had just told them the same thing. I began to sort out the areas in which I felt most competent and those where I sought consultation from Jim. I looked for patterns in Jim's selection of patients he wanted me to follow up and those I referred to him.

Then I happened upon *Knowing Woman* by Irene Claremont de Castillejo, a Jungian analyst. I was captivated by it immediately. Castillejo, following Jung, suggested that "on the whole the basic masculine attitude to life is that of focus, division and change; and the feminine (in either sex) is more nearly an attitude of acceptance, an awareness of the unity of all life and a readiness for relationship…. Today, when masculine and feminine characteristics are so interwoven in people of both sexes, it may be clearer to speak of 'focused consciousness' on the one hand and 'diffuse awareness' on the other, knowing that these qualities belong to both men and women in varying degrees."[2]

Although I knew little about Jungian psychology, I found this rough classification consistent with my own life experience. I wondered if it could be extrapolated to the health professions as well, for it had begun to seem to me that scientific medicine could be characterized as a masculine mode of healing and nursing as its counterpart, that is, healing in a feminine mode. This would explain how physician and nurse could have the same goal—healing—but approach it in different ways even while performing parallel or complementary functions much of the time.

Jim and me posing for a PR shot

I pictured a continuum with a masculine pole at one end and a feminine pole at the other. I placed medicine at the masculine pole and characterized it by problem solving, that is, the application of analytical techniques and medical technology to the identification and treatment of discrete medical problems. At the feminine pole I placed nursing and, after much thought and with some reservations about the adequacy of the term, characterized it by nurturing, a concept beyond caring that best describes the process by which nurses put patients in touch with their own strengths and potential for health while at the same time letting them draw temporarily on those of the nurse. Just as masculine and feminine characteristics are interwoven in all people, so problem solving and nurturing are characteristic of both physicians and nurses to varying degrees. For example, an ICU nurse might function close to the masculine or problem solving pole and a pediatrician or family physician, close to the feminine or nurturing pole. However, the major contribution of the nurse to healing a patient is likely to be in the realm of nurturing and that of the physician, in problem solving.

As I worked with the problem solving-nurturing dyad and with the idea of the healing continuum, other semantic dyads began to occur to me. One of the most important has proved to be technology-time. I was forced to come to grips with the fact that `time is as fundamental to nursing as technology is to medicine` when I first read the statistic Jim had quoted in a report on the state of our practice: according to the U.S. Department of Health and Human Services, one

> The difference between medicine and nursing is
> the difference between a pill and a presence,
> between technology and teaching. It is the differ-
> ence between a house call and a home visit.

nurse practicing in a primary care setting is equal to one-half a doctor. My immediate reaction was outrage. As I reckoned with the offending fraction, however, I realized that its significance was economic. All I had to do was to look at our office schedule. Over the months, we had evolved a practice of scheduling patients to see Jim at fifteen-minute intervals and me at thirty-minute intervals. Therefore, Jim saw twice as many patients and generated twice as much income as I did. At first I thought to myself that I would eventually get "better" and work faster. This was not the case. My approach to patients and their problems simply requires more time for listening, counseling, and teaching than does Jim's. I believe this is true for nurses in general. The difference between medicine and nursing is the difference between a pill and a presence, between technology and teaching. It is the difference between a house call and a home visit. In large part, it is the difference between obstetrics and midwifery.

Whereas medicine is based on the use of tools, nursing is based on the use of self: to listen, teach, guide, support, be there. You can design, standardize, and automate tools to achieve efficacy and speed. The self, on the other hand, cannot be streamlined, packaged, or delivered. Its effective use requires time, quality time.

Even our language tells us a truth about doctors and nurses as healers. When you doctor a drink, what do you do? You put something into it, altering it in some way. And when you nurse a drink, what do you do? You don't do anything to it! You spend time with it, appreciate it, linger over it. When nurses strike over the issue of staffing in their institutions, they are usually doing so to preserve their opportunity to nurse. When time is lacking, they are able to perform only those functions that revolve around medications, medically prescribed procedures, and machines. Important as these are, they are not enough. The simple fact is that nursing is time-dependent. Depriving a nurse of time is equivalent to depriving a physician of his laboratory and pharmacy, or a surgeon of his operating suite.

Another dyad that I have found useful in contrasting medicine and nursing is rule out-rule in. Typically, a physician focuses on the diseased part or system and asks the question: What does this case have in common with all others and how can it be classified? A nurse is more likely to look at the diseased part in the context of the whole person. She asks the question: How is this person unique?

On those occasions when Jim and I are seeing a patient in tandem, I find that he will start with the chief complaint and move deliberately to identify related signs and symptoms that can be grouped together and fitted into an established disease category with specific treatment options. I, too, take notice of the chief complaint, but tend to cast a wide net, searching out the possible relevance of everything from the symptom that doesn't fit to the history that cannot be substantiated to the oddities of a patient's story. I am loath to rule anything out.

I observe a related phenomenon at the day care center for the impaired elderly where I provide health supervision. New participants

HEALING	
Masculine Mode ←——→	Feminine Mode
Medicine ←——→	Nursing
Problem Solving ←——→	Nurturing
Technology ←——→	Time
Use of Tools ←——→	Use of Self
Rule Out ←——→	Rule In
Diseased Part ←——→	Whole Person
Logic ←——→	Intuition
Base in Physical & Life Sciences ←——→	Base in Humanities & Social Sciences
Universal Applicability ←——→	Culture-bound
Prescription ←——→	Mediation
Value on Autonomy ←——→	Value on Interdependence
Clearly Definable ←——→	Hard to Define

submit a medical evaluation form when they enter the program. After allowing time for participants to adjust to the center and for me to observe them I conduct a nursing assessment. Mr. Malloy's medical report listed his medical problems (left hemiplegia due to a stroke, glaucoma, hypertension), physical examination findings, and current medications. My assessment listed Mr. Malloy's own concerns about his health (a painful bunion on his right foot, not being able to drive), information about what he eats, how he sleeps, hears, and sees, his limitations, his spirits—even what he says he does to keep healthy. It is largely subjective and highly personal with many of my notes in the form of direct quotations. Which of the two is most useful? Both, say the staff members. You need the subjective and the objective, **the person and his problems.**

To diagnose and to heal, you also need both logic and intuition: logic, a masculine quality in the Jungian sense, a system of reasoning either from or to the known, a tool of science; and intuition, a quality of the feminine, the act of knowing without the use of rational processes, more a gift than a tool, but one that is most useful when tempered by a deep understanding of a person or situation.[3]

Expert physicians as well as expert nurses rely on intuition, but nurses' intuitions are frequently denigrated, perhaps because we experience more difficulty translating them into words. A nurse colleague told me about a chief resident she knew who admonished the house staff to go to the ward any time a nurse phoned one of them to say that she thought a patient was in trouble. He knew the nursing staff, he said, and he trusted their judgment. "No matter if they can't tell you why you should come. They know when something's wrong, so get down there." The resident was not merely tolerant; he was wise. He was able to appreciate that knowledge is not always reached through induction or deduction and it does not always lend itself to words. Certainly all physicians and nurses are articulate to varying degrees and the ability to articulate is valued by both professions.

That good nursing relies more heavily on intuition
may stem from the fact that it is rooted in the humanities and social sciences, the study of that which can
be appreciated or felt rather than known. In contrast,
modern medicine is grounded in the physical and life
sciences, the study of that which can be explained.
It has more to do with the laws of nature than the nature of humankind.

For that reason, too, medicine can be exported across cultural
and national boundaries while nursing is culture-bound, a
lesson I learned well while working in the field of international health.
Techniques of problem solving and applications of technology are easily
transplanted into contrasting cultures and universally understood by
those who speak the language of science. The practice of nursing cannot
be lifted out of its cultural context, nor can it always be understood
except in terms of the individual nurse-patient relationship.

There is a reticence characteristic of nursing that has nothing to do
with uncertainty or lack of assurance. It has to do with the nurse's role
as mediator as contrasted with that of the physician, which is to prescribe.
Most people go to the doctor in search of a mandate: Take this, do that,
come back then. They are not fully satisfied with less. On those occasions
when I have tried on the prescribing role, I have found it a poor fit. It is
not because I have trouble making decisions, but rather because I am satisfied only when my patient has chosen for himself. I will present options,
help a person to weigh them, challenge them and, finally, choose or reject
them. Sometimes a patient will become frustrated because her expectations have not been met: "But you're supposed to tell me what to do!"
And so I suggest, then wait for the suggestion to be accepted or rejected.

In the course of my work at CMC, I have learned that mediation
and prescription are complementary functions. Ideally, Jim
prescribes and sets direction. I mediate and give
freedom and support. When Jim prescribes a regimen for a newly

diagnosed diabetic, I am at my best gauging the patient's reaction, elicit-
ing questions and concerns, filling in details, teaching techniques, assessing the level of motivation to carry out the regimen, and involving family
and others in the plan of care.

In these days of strikes, standoffs, and assertiveness training, it may
come as a surprise to many that **nurses value interdependence
above autonomy.** "That's not what I've been hearing," one physician
said to me. Nevertheless, it's true. For most physicians, autonomy means
a private practice as free as possible from governmental, organizational,
and legal constraints. When consultation occurs among physicians, there
is always the caveat that each will protect the autonomy of the other.
Nurses want autonomy of a different kind. They want to make decisions
and act on them within their area of expertise, they want to be paid
directly and appropriately for the services they provide, and a very few
want to practice independently. Left to themselves and given due respect
for their abilities, they will make it their business to consult and defer,
when appropriate, to the expertise of others. Nurses have always relied
upon their teammates to help them turn, calm, or treat difficult patients;
they depend on their colleagues to continue the care of their patients
through the day, evening, and night shifts. They are most often the ones
who call in the dietician, physical therapist, visiting nurse, social worker,
family, chaplain, friendly visitor. Interdependence is a fact of life in
both nursing and medicine. The difference is that it is likely to be chosen
by nurses but grudgingly accepted by doctors.

The last dyad was not one I thought to include. It was proposed by
Jim when I presented this schema to him for the first time. **Medicine,**
he suggested, **is rather easily and clearly defined; nursing is intrinsically hard to define.** He is right, as those
of us nurses who have struggled to define what we do will be the first
to admit. Castillejo says that the "inability to find words is one of the
outstanding characteristics of the feminine."[4] For those whose ways

of healing take them beyond the realm of the rational, it should come as no surprise that servants of the intellect, such as words, cannot always accompany them there.

Having tried to explain nursing and medicine as complementary modes of healing, I must now say something about my motive for doing so. I do not feel any more disposed to prescribe for the nursing profession than I do for my patients, but I cannot resist this opportunity to nurse it along. As we all know, most healing takes place without benefit of professional intervention. There are, however, two prototype healers sanctioned by our society: nurses and doctors. In the past, doctors were better nurses, perhaps because in a humanistic age before the ascendancy of technology—and nursing—they had the time, inclination, and social mandate to be so. That time is gone. We are a society in love with science and we demand the cures we believe technology can provide. We have charged the medical profession with dominating ever-accelerating technical advances. At the same time, we feel something is missing in medical care. Our physician does not always hear us out, does not seem interested in our less challenging complaints, does not really know us on a personal basis; he may not even know anything about our bodies beyond the system that is his particular concern. This is not only regrettable, it impedes healing.

What people are missing in modern medicine is modern nursing. Yet, as the feminine mode of healing, it is undervalued by society and sometimes by nurses themselves. This must not be. Put simply, the object of nursing is health. It follows that the principal function of nurses is healing. Healing happens in many ways, most of which elude cause and effect analysis. Only one thing is sure: that physicians and nurses working together with a clear sense of their individual and professional strengths and limitations have potential for healing the whole person unequaled by either healer alone.

This is from a piece Jim wrote for the annual report, one of many that include parables from the natural world. I was captivated by the image of the nurse log and the metaphor it provides for professional nursing.

The ancient rain forest in the Hoh River Valley on the western slope of Mt. Olympus in Washington State is a long way from Community Medical Care in Washington, DC. Ask any of us who made the "great trip west" by car this past summer. Or ask the man behind the counter at a fresh produce market in Yakima who had trouble finding Washington, DC, on the large U.S. map behind him. Yet, standing in that ancient forest so far from home in front of the fallen trunk of a huge old Douglas fir, I was brought up short by the words of our trip leader. Gesturing toward the fallen fir trunk he said, "This is a nurse log."

The nurse log of which I speak…is not a list of patients being kept by a dutiful nurse. Nor is it a member of that esteemed profession with an unusual last name. No, the log of which I speak is an integral part of the ecology of the ancient forest. As this old, dead tree begins to decompose on the forest floor, it provides the ideal place for seedlings of new trees to grow. From atop the old log they send branches up and roots down. Even after decay has claimed all traces of the old log, a straight row of young trees of similar age, reaching toward the canopy, will mark its place. We learn that no forest, rain forest or otherwise, is really mature or complete without the old dead trees that nourish new trees. Such is the ecology of the forest— a circle of renewal and healing.

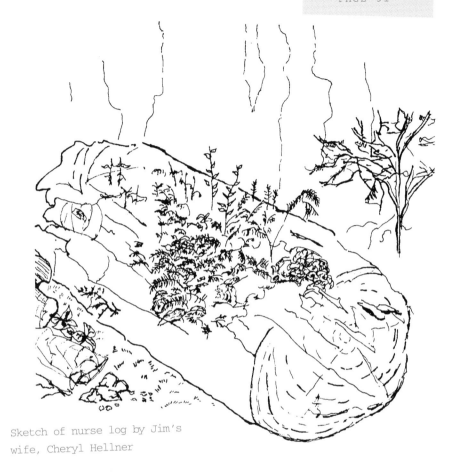

Sketch of nurse log by Jim's
wife, Cheryl Hellner

In the days since that day in the Hoh rain forest the image of the
nurse log has pursued me. In idle moments I have wondered: if there are
nurse logs are there doctor logs? No one I have consulted, neither forester
or forest, has ever seen a doctor log. In my frustration I have tried to
imagine such a log. When disaster strikes the forest, the doctor log springs
into action, propping up the tottering tulip trees, wrapping itself around
the wounded willows, and rushing to save the sycamores. But in truth, the
forest knows no doctor logs, knows only nurse logs...

When we were invited to contribute an article to an issue on primary health care in the World Health Organization's magazine, *World Health*, Jim, Katrina, Sharon, and I spoke in our own voices as physician, health aide, patient care coordinator, and nurse. Interestingly, Teresa, who would join our staff as nurse practitioner a few years later, first heard about CMC when she happened upon this article.

Poverty and disease, like health and wealth, seem to go together. We associate the former with some nations and the latter with others. In the United States, a very wealthy nation, total health care expenditures in 1980 amounted to...close to ten percent of the gross national product. Surely so much money should be sufficient to put health within the reach of every citizen.

But money cannot always buy a cure or even compassionate health care. And those who do not have money to pay are less likely than those who do to have their health needs met by the complicated mosaic of health institutions and services in the United States. In a great city like Washington, DC, there are many whose options are limited by poverty, immobility, or hopelessness. Bringing healing to some of these people has been the aim of Community Medical Care (CMC), a venture in primary health care within the context of the U.S. health system.

CMC is a private, nonprofit corporation formed in 1978 to provide family health care in home and office settings for a poor neighborhood of Washington about a mile from the Capitol Building. It is governed by a board of directors and run by a four-person team whose efforts are supplemented by a small number of volunteers and part-time paid staff members. The 1981 operating budget of $65,000 was raised in part by fees for service charged on a sliding scale according to a person's income and number of dependents. Approximately 50 percent of the total income came in the form of reimbursements from such bodies as Medicare (government health insurance for the elderly) and Medicaid (government health insurance for people on public assistance). CMC serves about 1,500 people of all ages from a variety of races, cultural backgrounds, and income levels.

Since the story of CMC, how it came to be, and how it functions now may be of interest to communities far removed from Washington, DC, the four of us who make up the health team have decided to tell it in our own words.

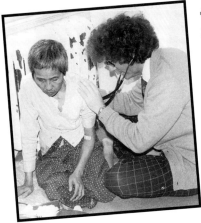

PHOTO: ANITA CARTON

James Hall, Physician

Several years ago, some church friends suggested that I start a general medical clinic in a low-income neighborhood in Washington, DC. Being of an academic turn of mind, I started to review the literature on this sort of thing and kept running across the term "primary health care."

How do you do primary health care, I wondered? The answers seemed to come largely from the sphere of international health. The more I read, the more the health problems in the so-called third world countries seemed to be similar to those in inner-city Washington. Perhaps ideas like "houses of health," "barefoot doctors," and "health by the people" could teach us some things about providing primary health care in North America, I thought.

And so we began doing primary care, utilizing some basic principles drawn from the international experience. These principles include the significant use of para-professional staff drawn from the neighborhood, an extensive home care outreach program involving the entire clinic staff, a strong emphasis on continuing health education for staff and patients, and a holistic view of health as encompassing the social, emotional, and spiritual as well as physical dimensions of health. These principles, along with our base in a church community and regular worship and prayer together, are what have shaped our particular venture in health care.

A short time ago, I was sitting on the floor of a small room in an upstairs flat with a Southeast Asian refugee family. We were seated on the floor as is the custom in Cambodia. With me were Veneta (our nurse), a nursing student, and an interpreter from the Indochinese Refugee Center. Several months earlier, the father had come to our office quite depressed about his lack of employment and his wife's illness. Subsequently, we determined that his wife had tuberculosis but had somehow slipped through the cracks of the local health care system and had not been treated.

By the time of our visit, she was under our care and feeling better, though still in pain from swollen lymph glands that I had drained in the office the week before. She needed comfort and some further education about the nature of her illness and its communicability. Others in the family needed tests and lesser treatment. As they shared with us some photographs from the Thai Refugee Camp where they had been interned and from a wedding, life seemed to grow more cheerful. And I couldn't help thinking that, yes, right here, here is how you do primary health care.

Veneta Masson, Nurse

When I first heard Jim Hall talk about his vision of health care for one of Washington's neighborhoods, I was busily engaged as Director of Nursing for Project Hope, a voluntary organization engaged in international health activities. I traveled, I planned programs for and with nurses from many other countries, and I learned to see health from an international perspective. Distanced as I was becoming from health needs and services in my own country and city, I began to wonder how concepts such as primary health care and the village health worker—concepts I bandied about in conversations all the time—might apply here in the United States. I also realized how much I wanted the opportunity to practice nursing again and to accept the challenge of meeting the health needs of individuals rather than those of an anonymous aggregate.

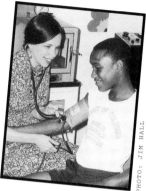

PHOTO: JIM HALL

On a limited basis at first, and eventually full-time when I resigned from my administrative position, I worked with Jim and others to create what came to be known as Community Medical Care.

In the beginning, I was interested and not a little anxious to discover how Jim and I would work together. I thought that what I did as the nurse might prove different and distinct from what he did as the physician. I supposed that I would be the expert at health teaching, counseling, creating an environment in which healing could take place, and building a person's own capacities to achieve health—in short, nurturing—while he would excel at applying medical technologies to the solution of discrete medical problems. As time went on, I realized that there was no clear-cut difference in our roles. Rather there seemed to be a continuum with what I have called nurturing at one end and problem solving at the other. In any given situation, either of us might be functioning at any point along this continuum. For example, I might be treating a person with an upper respiratory infection and Jim might be counseling the mother of a young child. Generally speaking, however, I found that my gifts tended to lie in the area of nurturing and his in problem solving, so that when we worked together, there was a complementarity of healing modes.

Of course, Jim and I do not function in a vacuum. Both Sharon and Katrina are an integral part of the CMC team, and our individual contributions have become difficult to describe separately. Although Katrina is the health aide, for many of our patients she is the nurse, the team member who satisfies their expectations of what a nurse is and does. And Sharon is often heard explaining how to handle common illnesses or listening to the chatter and lament of a chronically ill elder. As for me, I am learning simply to respond to whatever is called for, to do what needs to be done, and to take great satisfaction in seeing many of our patients move a few steps closer to health.

Katrina Gibbons, Health Aide

My job as health aide at Community Medical Care started in September 1978. I was looking for a permanent job because the training program in which I was working was coming to an end. The director of the program informed us that there was a job as health aide with Dr. Hall. I was interviewed for this job and was hired.

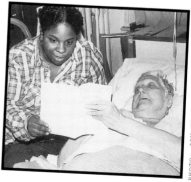

As the health aide at CMC, my duties are to take patients' vital signs, heights and weights. I prepare them for examinations and assist with minor surgery and lab work. I also make home visits and do electrocardiograms.

PHOTO: JIM HALL

I have had several personal experiences with our patients. We had been caring for an elderly brother and sister from Russia, Vera and Vlodya. Vera needed someone to help her in the evenings because both she and Vlodya were ill and confined to bed. So I would leave work and go straight to her apartment. There I would prepare dinner, get Vlodya into the wheelchair, and bring him to the table. Vera would come too, and I would serve them both and feed him. Vlodya was ninety-six years old and very withdrawn. After several months of close contact, he became more open with me. Once I had to take him to the hospital. We were in the emergency room for about three hours, waiting, when Vlodya finally shouted out loudly and in plain English, "I would like to order two well-done pork chop sandwiches, please!" I was somewhat embarrassed at first, then I comforted him with a piece of chocolate candy until he was safe and secure in a hospital room. He stayed there for about a week and then returned home. Finally he caught pneumonia and died at home in his bed in September 1981. Because Vera could not get out to attend a funeral service, we planned one at CMC, keeping it plain and simple, and held it in the apartment. I will always treasure the memory and tender moments with Vlodya.

Sharon Baskerville, Patient Care Coordinator

I first became involved with CMC as a patient. I happened upon a brochure advertising the presence of a new neighborhood clinic which was located just around the corner from where I lived. I tucked the brochure away for future reference and, being the mother of three small children, found need to avail myself of the clinic's services the following week. Taking my son to the clinic for treatment for a simple infection opened up a whole new chapter in the life of myself and my family. I was so impressed by the attitude of the staff, the compassion, and the quality of care that I soon became a fervent supporter of CMC.

A few months later, a position as receptionist opened, and Jim Hall sent me a job application with a brief "Sharon, thought you might be interested" written across the top. What an understatement!

I started by doing twelve hours a week at the front desk, checking in patients, making appointments, filing, and answering the phone. Later, I took on the responsibilities of business manager and increasingly, as the need presented itself, became the unofficial social worker, information and referral service, and jack of all trades. To cover this mixture of activities, we came up with my present job title of patient care coordinator. It is now a full-time position.

PHOTO: JIM HALL

Most people view the job at the front desk of a medical facility as primarily clerical and made up of routine tasks. I think, because of our particular approach to medical care, that we function as a team, a body if you will, with each member functioning as a separate but equally vital organ of that body. I see the front desk as the heart of our activity. Although routine tasks abound, I often have the opportunity to glean information relevant to the care of the patient which might not be given in the more formal setting of the examining room. I am often privy to the day to day struggles of our patients, the joys, the sorrows, triumphs, and failures, things that they feel are too trivial to mention to the doctor or nurse. These things are often vitally important to our overall understanding of the person and can directly influence the type of care plan evolved.

As evidence of our "whole being" approach to medical care, we, the staff, have become a sort of extended family to many of our patients. True, some view us as just a source of relief or treatment for an acute medical problem, but a great number of our patients look on us as an integral part of their lives. Thus we are invited to share in the celebration of birthdays and weddings; we are also sought out for consolation in times of sorrow or mourning.

I've had the opportunity here at CMC to be both a recipient and a provider, to be on both sides of the desk, so to speak. The desire I had as a patient was to be treated as a whole person, not just as a diagnostic problem, to participate in my own health care, to be cared for and comforted when the need arose. This is what I have tried to do for the patients that we serve.

In Conclusion

It would still be premature to promote the CMC model as one which could easily be adopted and adapted by others. After three and a half years, we are still not fully self-supporting, in part because such a large proportion of our patients pay below cost, and also because some of the services we provide (supportive counseling and certain types of home nursing, for example) are not reimbursed by government health insurance schemes. Home care takes time away from the potentially more cost-efficient office practice. Some of our patients, out of habit, still revert to hospital emergency rooms for acute problems after clinic hours, although we can be reached twenty-four hours a day.

On the whole, however, the CMC experiment is working. We often help people to avoid the need to be admitted to a hospital. (We recently reversed the course of congestive heart failure in an acutely ill octogenarian for less than $300 in physician and nurse visits, drugs, laboratory tests, and electrocardiograms. That is less than half the cost of one day in a hospital intensive care unit.) Continuity of care is maintained. Liaison with other community agencies has been established.

And many of our patients tell us we have helped them. Shelley Stancil is one of them. She describes herself in these words: "I'm a single parent of three school-aged children. My family subsists on public assistance. I am certifiably, undeniably poor." And this is what she says about Community Medical Care: "I think more clinics like CMC should spring up, where drug addicts and prostitutes are treated with the same respect as businessmen, where people are treated holistically. I think public health services need to come out of themselves, as it were, and to assess themselves to determine what their objectives are and determine if they are truly attaining them. I believe that all people have God-given rights, among them the right to respect and dignity. For God made us all and He didn't make no junk!"

Most people cling so tenaciously to their belief in the power of medicine that they are blind to the healing that comes through nursing. Max was one of them.

Not long ago, walking down a street in the neighborhood where I work, I came up behind a small knot of people, their backs turned to me. Hearing a familiar male voice, I tuned in to a snatch of conversation that went like this: "Yeah, I feel a whole lot better. I went to see the doctor and got a prescription...." When I realized that the voice I was hearing belonged to Max Settles, I stifled an impulse to tap him on the shoulder and ask, "What do you mean, you went to the doctor and got a prescription and now you feel better?" Instead, I tossed off a casual greeting and went my way. After all, there was truth in what Max had said. A long-time patient in our family practice, he had indeed been in to see us a week ago. He left with a prescription. But he had not seen the physician. His appointment—his last several, in fact—had been with me, his nurse.

Max is in his early sixties, retired on disability with chronic conditions that include hypertension and diabetes. He takes more than one prescription medicine "pretty regularly," but has difficulty controlling his weight, his diet ("You can't take everything away from a person," he maintains), and stresses related to family, finances, and the transition from breadwinner to pensioner.

What happened during Max's office visit? I spent thirty minutes with him. To an observer, the encounter might have seemed casual. We joked a little. I listened to how he felt. I answered his questions in a way that I hoped made sense in terms of his personal experience of health and illness. I reminded him of the things he could do to exert some control over his symptoms and prognosis. I checked his weight, blood pressure, and urine and blood glucose, sharing the findings with him as we went along. "Hmm, maybe I'm still eating too much," he said, reflecting on his high blood sugar reading and his two-pound weight gain.

"When do you think you should come back?" I asked as the encounter came to an end. "Oh, about a month, I guess," he answered. "Fair enough," I said, adding, "Do you need refills on your medicines? Can you afford to get the prescriptions filled now, or will you have to wait until your next check comes? Okay, take care and I'll look for you in a month."

"Bye, Doc," Max said as he headed back to the reception area.

Sure, Max knows I'm a nurse. He'll admit it if I press him on the point. But he is no different from the majority of our patients. Down deep, he believes that it is medicine that heals. Everybody knows that doctors are the ones who prescribe medicines. Therefore, the person who gives you a prescription is doctoring. It's as simple as that.

Sharon, our patient care coordinator, sometimes takes a phone call from a new person asking for an appointment with the doctor. "Doctor Hall doesn't have any appointments open for the next few days," she says when that's the case. "Would you like to make an appointment with the nurse?"

"Can she write prescriptions?" the caller wants to know. "Yes? Well, then, that'll be all right."

There was a time when I, too, believed that what heals is medicine or surgery or procedures with long, Latinate names, and that the laying on of hands, the giving of information and counsel, listening, comforting, and inspiriting were important but ancillary. Now I know that while this is true in some cases, in others it is the reverse. But most people, like Max, cling so tenaciously to their belief in the power of medicine that they are blind to the healing that comes through nursing.

Why else would someone feel better after a surgical procedure that had no demonstrable effect on the problem that precipitated it? Why else would a patient tell me that without the flu shot, he just wouldn't be able to make it through the winter? Why does patient after patient produce stunning collections of capsules, pills, creams, sprays and drops without which, they are fully convinced, they would be reduced to a quivering mass of symptoms?

I have come to understand that people need to be doctored as well as nursed and that the most effective doctors and nurses learn to do some of both.

A year or two ago, I ordered some printed forms, larger than a prescription pad, but designed to carry the same weight in the eyes of the recipient even though the forms say Veneta Masson, RN, instead of James Hall, MD, at the top. On them, I write pertinent information about the diagnosis (giving a name for what is wrong is part of the treatment), self-care instructions, and follow-up plans. I prepare these

VENETA MASSON, R.N., M.A.
COMMUNITY MEDICAL CARE
1118 NINTH ST. NW
WASHINGTON, DC 20001
202-234-0333

*You have viral pharyngitis.
You may take 2 aspirin or
Tylenol every four hours
for pain. Keep your throat moist. Drink
lots of fluids. Suck on lozenges on hand*

with care, hand them to the patient with a certain amount of ceremony, and then go over what I've written with them.

The other day, I got a phone call from a puzzled pharmacist. One of our patients had put in her prescription to be filled, but it wasn't at all clear to the pharmacist what had been prescribed. "Why don't you read it to me," I suggested. This is what he read:

You have viral pharyngitis.

You may take 2 aspirins or Tylenol every four hours for pain.

Keep your throat moist. Drink lots of fluids.

Suck on lozenges or hard candy.

Get plenty of rest.

Phone tomorrow for the result of your throat culture.

Come back in 2 days if you are not feeling better.

"Put Mrs. Moore on the phone," I sighed, "and let me explain it to her again."

The undertakers already do a brisk business in this
part of the city. What, I asked myself, is left to be
reaped by the whirlwind of AIDS?

The article in the Wall Street Journal hit me between the eyes. It wasn't
that the subject was AIDS. Nor that it was about AIDS in Washington,
DC. What hit was the focus on AIDS in the neighborhood where I
work — "a Washington slum called 'the Graveyard,' " according to the
headline.

"More and more, AIDS is threatening to overwhelm inner-city
people, who already endure enough hardship," I read. "Some say it is
only a matter of time before the most important occupations at 8th and
M — prostitution and drug dealing — are supplanted by the work of
undertakers."[5]

The undertakers already do a brisk business in this part of the city,
what with untimely deaths from untreated illness, drugs, violence,
and accidents. What, I asked myself, is left to be reaped by the whirlwind
of AIDS?

Perhaps I've grown used to working in the place I think of as "real
life," where poverty is physical, not just spiritual, where thanks is given
not for achievements and opportunities, but for survival, where hope
is fixed on striking it rich in the lottery, and fate deals many blows that
seem as cruel as AIDS.

Certainly Community Medical Care, my clinic, has been affected by
the AIDS epidemic. Some of our patients and acquaintances in the
neighborhood have died from it. One was Nick, who, according to his
old medical records, had enlarged lymph nodes as early as 1982. He died
of cryptococcal meningitis in 1986, a year after he became our patient.

There was Mr. Lightly, a deferent, smiling, sixty-year-old homosexual, who had been picked up more than once for selling his insulin syringes to drug users at the corner of 11th and O. His health was failing. He began to lose weight. His bloodwork indicated the need to begin a workup for AIDS. Some days after his last office visit, he was found dead in his apartment. We do not know exactly why he died.

There's Wilma, who burst into the waiting room after her most recent discharge from St. Elizabeth's, the psychiatric hospital. Throwing her arms around Sharon at the front desk, she proclaimed for all to hear, "They say I got the virus, but I don't have the disease!" We are supposed to be checking her Lithium levels every month despite the problems of achieving venipuncture in her drug-scarred veins.

There are the worried ones. The Hispanic woman who wonders if the fatigue of unrelenting domestic work plus the care of her own large family is the first sign of AIDS. The girlfriend of an IV drug user who has watched him growing thin and weak. "I've stopped sleeping with him," she says, "but it might be too late."

20 **THE WALL STREET JOURNAL** WEDNESDAY, NOVEMBER 4, 1987

Mean Streets: AIDS Brings Death To a Neighborhood of Suffering

Continued From First Page

someone who has been touched by the disease.

One man, nicknamed Dog, has seen two friends die of AIDS in just the past few weeks. Francine, who like others in the neighborhood is unwilling to give her last name, was close to two people who died, and she says she has seen many familiar [faces grow] thin and sickly. [A man] on intrave-

denial creates a group difficult to reach with messages imploring condom use and other so-called safer-sex techniques. Meanwhile, women who are intimate with bisexual men can become unsuspecting conduits to other heterosexuals, as can women who go to bed with needle users.

Needing Condoms

"You've got to tell these people they need to wear condoms," says Adrianne Blackwell, an outspoken community activist, a 23-year-old transvestite who serves [a] black gay bar.

And there's Len. His was the first positive HIV test I drew. Len is not from the clinic neighborhood. He is an expensively dressed, engaging and sophisticated university student—one of a group of patients who seem to feel our location is sufficiently obscure that they can be assured of anonymous diagnosis and treatment of their socially unacceptable health problems. Len had phoned to make an appointment for sinusitis, but once in the examining room it did not take him long to reveal the real reason for his visit. He had just turned over a new leaf, he said. He and his new male lover had made a commitment to give up cocaine and promiscuity in order to concentrate on their studies and build a healthy life together. The first step was to confirm that both were free of AIDS. Yes, he understood about false positives, false negatives. No, there was no doubt about wanting to take the test, no matter what it might reveal.

Back in our office a few days later, Len got the bad news. Visibly shaken, he asked a few questions and was gone. Then he came back, again and again—once with his mother, a physician, for a conference with our physician. He still phones regularly for information and advice. He is planning his life in light of the possibility of continued health, or of progressive illness and death. At least he has options, people who care about him, financial security.

Len's reaction to his positive HIV test was of a different order from that of the majority of our patients. For them, AIDS is a source of fear or a reason for denial, but there is little surprise, little motivation to change behavior or plan for the future. They are the same men and women who can't seem to practice birth control, who come in with one sexually transmitted infection after the other, who do drugs, who can't do the things they know to do to keep themselves and their families healthy. Unsafe sex, drug and alcohol abuse, unemployment, poverty, and homelessness or near-homelessness are the facts of their lives. They do not believe they can control anything that happens to them.

How different is my philosophy, I wonder, when people ask what precautions I'm taking against AIDS at the clinic. Do you wear gloves when you draw blood? is a favorite question. No, I say. Are you warning your patients? Yes, I say, but not with any conviction that it will make a difference.

Then came the article in the Wall Street Journal. It begins and ends on a note of despair, the same despair that I realize has characterized my own feeling about AIDS in our neighborhood. What will be will be. Nevertheless, the article provoked me to action. If I as a nurse have nothing to offer but complicity in despair, I am doing nothing to create an environment in which health is a possibility. I am not nurturing, not lending or engendering strength.

We've begun to think creatively about AIDS in our clinic staff meetings. I've also started telephoning around town. Here we are, I say, what can we do? How and what can we teach in the course of routine office visits? Will informational literature be helpful or not? Do we get out into the neighborhood instead of waiting for it to come to us? Would giving out free condoms reinforce the message of safe sex, at least among the young? What precautions should we ourselves take?

I am changing my behavior and attitude about AIDS. Whether my patients will be able to change theirs is another question. At least they will know that we have something to offer them: hope in the midst of despair and faith in the ability of a seemingly helpless person to change.

Sharon wrote a long, poignant poem for the annual
report—a prayer for a woman and child who
were our patients and for herself as caregiver.
What follows is an excerpt.

And the tears unwept, unwept, unwept
through the years
well up

Whenever I, in prayer, bring my pain to you.
Pain hidden carefully under
kind words,
gentle strokes,
hard-edged humor,
playful admonishments,
whispered loving words
that come from
where?

The torrent,
the rush of pain I feel
when not on guard,
when not in service,
when not in this work
you asked of me.

And the tears unwept, unwept, unwept
through the years
well up

As I hold Rhonda over the toilet as she vomits up the bile
of her life and whimpers,
as I rub my hands over her swollen belly and feel
the rounded rump of her fifth child-to-be
pushing
straining
against taut, smooth skin,
doing the bump and grind
as I murmur prayers of protection and love and healing
as I wipe her mouth and help her out to a waiting stretcher
as I walk beside, holding her hand, to the ambulance
as I wonder fleetingly if the red stuff in the basin of retch
from her gut
was it blood?
her virus-tainted blood?
do I have any cuts?
as I hear that she's on the street again
where he knocks her down
and does those unspeakable things,
as she shows up on Friday night at closing
for the things she left
the day the ambulance took her away,
as she says, "Don't worry, I'm gonna do what you said."

My eyes are dry

Till I come to you in prayer

And the tears unwept, unwept, unwept
through the years
well up...

It was one of the hardest tasks we had set ourselves as a staff, the more so because we tried to look only at ourselves, our needs, and our contributions to the clinic without reference to education, status, or market forces.

Put yourself into this scene: it's time to prepare next year's budget. The staff of your organization have filed into a room. Each of you knows the projected budget figure for the year and the sum available for salaries—the salary pie. Each of you has been asked to come with a plan for slicing that pie, your piece and a piece for each of your colleagues. Each person will explain how he or she believes the pie should be divided, and then the group will have to reach consensus on the final cut. Today.

Incredible? Impractical? Probably. But I'll tell you how it happened in one small organization: Community Medical Care. If your reaction to the challenge of slicing the salary pie is like ours, you don't want to go to that meeting. It's so much easier to let someone else do the slicing and then complain about the size of your piece. Besides, would you want to reveal all the rational and irrational forces that guide your hand and mind as you slice? It might be okay to say how large your own slice should be, but it's exceedingly uncomfortable to take responsibility for how your cut will affect what is left for the others. It is a zero-sum game, after all. What I win, you lose, and vice versa. Everything you have ever heard or thought about what you are worth compared to the other people rushes through your head.

So who filed into the conference room at Community Medical Care and what happened to the salary pie? There was Jim, the physician; Kathy, the social worker; Sharon, the patient care coordinator; Edy, the medical assistant; and me, the nurse and director. It was a very small budget and a very small salary pie. Still, no one wanted to make the first cut. Low rumblings about raises past due, one person's salary in relation to another's, and who works harder and longer than whom surfaced as uneasy jokes. Throats cleared, papers unfolded and refolded. One by one we took our turn, said as much as we could of what we had come prepared to say.

When all the cards had been placed on the table, this is what we had:

Jim: seniority (CMC had been his idea), an MD degree that entitled us to clinic status and reimbursement from third-party payers, personal influence and professional authority within the organization, high market value, another part-time position with a good salary and benefits, two children to support, high premiums for professional liability insurance.

Veneta: seniority (a partner in the organization from the beginning), administrative as well as patient care responsibilities, ability to generate income for the clinic, no outside job, but what one colleague called "the economic subsidy of marriage," lower market value than Jim's.

Kathy: a part-timer with a private counseling practice of her own, not dependent on CMC for her livelihood, ability to generate income for CMC, market value comparable to Veneta's and a healthy regard for reimbursement as a reflection of professional status.

Sharon: seniority almost equal to Veneta's, and Jim's with a powerful personal position in the organization, unable to generate income directly but a magnet for drawing in patients, a husband on disability and children to support, no health insurance or retirement benefits with the exception of Social Security.

Edy: competent and growing in her position and participation in the organization but no direct income-generating power, able to attract new patients because of neighborhood contacts, a single parent raising three children, just off public assistance with no health insurance or retirement benefits except Social Security, no electricity in her apartment.

Until now, our salaries had spanned a relatively narrow range from high to low in the order our names are listed. Support staff (Sharon and

Edy) earned salaries at market rates while professional staff earned substantially below market because of our financial status as a nonprofit organization in a low-income neighborhood dependent on sliding-scale fees. Jim's salary was lower in comparison to the average for physicians than Kathy's and mine in comparison to the averages for nurses and social workers.

But who worked hardest? Who most efficiently? Who generated the most income, whether directly or indirectly? Who made the organization go? Who had the greatest need? The greatest claim? I had to confess that, ever since taking over the directorship, I had felt I should be earning as much as Jim, although my family finances were in better shape than his. But what about Sharon and Edy, with no health insurance, struggling to keep their families fed, clothed, and warm? How could my case for a raise compare with theirs?

In the end, most of what needed to be aired, was aired, and that in itself was therapeutic. We decided what changes to make, then I, as director, did the final juggling of dollars and cents. Jim's salary dropped (his initiative), but the clinic would pick up his professional liability insurance premiums. My salary edged up to equal his (although I knew I would be working many unpaid hours). Kathy received a smaller increase, reflecting the fact that she had less at stake. Sharon and Edy received the largest salary increases plus full health insurance coverage for their families.

It was one of the hardest tasks we had set ourselves as a staff, the more so because we tried to look only at ourselves, our needs, and our contributions to the organization without reference to educational preparation, professional status or market forces and without the constraints of tradition, agency, policy, or collective bargaining rituals.

It won't happen like that in any hospital, health department, HMO, home health agency, or private medical practice I know. But could it? And what if it did?

The following is from Jim's 1982 report as President of CMC's Board of Directors. It reflects on the move from our first "home" at Ninth & L Streets to a new location at Ninth & P. We were to stay at Ninth & P for eight years before moving back home.

It has been a year now since we arrived one morning to find a sign on our "old" clinic building reading "For Sale: Thomas Circle East — Luxury Office Condominiums." Initial amusement that our clinic was so elegantly renamed in the face of the abandoned and boarded up buildings all around, the trash in the street, and the varied clientele at the Chinese laundromat next door, soon gave way to a dull ache in the pit of our stomachs that was to remain there for most of the year. Hey, this is for real. Our landlord is selling the building. We're being displaced! To those of us not accustomed to life on the margin — on the bottom of the inner-city totem pole — the shock was a rude one indeed.

With something less than total enthusiasm, the search for a new site began, and eventually culminated in our finding a place in an excellent location just up the street from the old clinic. It was affordable, would be remodeled according to our specifications, and had a five-year lease which we signed with great relief.

Our relief lasted about as long as our amusement at the "Thomas Circle East" sign, for one early summer Friday found us with insufficient funds in the bank to make payroll. Anticipated returns from an extensive solicitation of many foundations had been meager. The summer months ahead were traditionally slow for both patient visits and contributions. Our loan sources were more interested in repayment than in new loans. It was therefore clear that we could no longer continue to spend $6000 each month while taking in $3500 and raising $2500. Consequently, we made some hard decisions, placing me on no-salary status, reducing the hours of our health aide, and eliminating the position of development coordinator. In that way we made it though the summer, living again close to the margin (in this case, economic) and breathed another sigh of relief.

Again, our relief was short lived. The real problem was just beginning. Originally scheduled to move to our new location on October 1, enigmatic construction delays kept pushing the date back: November 1, November 15, November 22, December 1, December 7 — creating

The "new" clinic at Ninth & P

a tremendous strain on us all and on our poor patients who never knew where to go for their return appointments. At last, the first weekend in January, after the new heating system was finally completed, staff and patients and their families gathered to move to the new site. All went well and we rested that Sunday while temperatures fell to below zero all over Washington, with rising winds.

Monday morning dawned clear and cold. Unfortunately, it was equally cold inside the new clinic where a thin film of ice had formed in the upstairs toilet...ice that sent a deep chill through us all. The good news and the bad news were the same: the furnace was working fine. The design of the heating system was not so fine, however, and it suddenly began to look like a long, cold winter ahead. What a lot of home visits we made that week! Space heaters and plumbers soon made their appearance and we were back in business...marginally, of course, especially considering that the underlying problem turned out to be that our landlord was nearly bankrupt (one could guess why) and the possibility that the building could go to foreclosure was (and is) very real...

I find it increasingly easy...to identify with the struggles of many, many of our patients because we've had to live with many of the same struggles....

With careful budgeting, our monthly income costs are slightly less than a year ago, even though I am back on salary. Our income per patient visit has risen from $11 to $16. And, after a marked drop in patient visits in January, there has been a steady rise. On paper, if we could sustain the number of patient visits per month that we reached last October (330), we would be self-supporting. But in fact, things never turn out quite as good as they look on paper, and I suspect that we may be a ministry on the margin for the foreseeable future....

In the clinic at Ninth & P, the business office was
upstairs. Downstairs was where we saw patients.
As director and clinician, I worked in both places.
This fact gave rise to a dilemma which, as usual,
revolved around money. (For the record, our budget
in 1980 was approximately $57,000. By 1995, it had
grown to $177,700.)

To understand the significance of upstairs, downstairs, you have to picture the layout of the clinic where I work. It is a two-story townhouse. Upstairs we have a room that passes for a business office. Downstairs is where we see patients. To understand the dilemma of upstairs, downstairs, you have to know that I work in both places — and sometimes I think I am two different people.

When I am upstairs, hunkered over the accounts or the quarterly financial report, the phone traffic between the two floors is usually brisk. "Sharon," I say (Sharon is patient care coordinator and works at the front desk downstairs), "Do you have a minute? I was just looking at the statement from National Health Labs. How in heaven's name could we have spent so much on lab in one month? Our lab income is nowhere near this figure." Sharon, who has already seen the statement, sighs. "Well," she says, "all those charges got there in the usual way. You see that big one for the Mendoza kids? You're the one who saw them, remember? You said they both had blood in their urine and needed lab tests. You told their mother you realized the children had just arrived from Salvador and that she had no money to pay, but we'd do them anyway. That was you."

"Oh," I answer. "Well, what about this beta Hcg quantitative?"

"Look at the name," Sharon replies coolly. "That was Donna's. You were afraid she might have an ectopic pregnancy. She told you she didn't get a Medicaid card this month and didn't have the money right then, but you said the bloodwork was important, so you sent it in."

"Oh," I say, recalling my decision.

"The bill's correct. I checked it. Do you have any more questions?" Sharon asks.

"No," I answer. "Talk to you later."

It's the same with office visit fees. "People have to pay something when they come or we won't see them — unless they're really ill," we preach to each other during staff meetings, each person ready to point a finger at another for violating the rule. "That's why we have a sliding scale. Besides, it's important for patients to take responsibility for their health care. It's a way of showing our respect for them," we say, nodding righteously.

It doesn't work out in practice. A look at the records for any week will show you that. And I'm as guilty as anyone else. Take Slim. I saw him on the street and he mentioned the ulcer on his foot. I urged him to come in and let us see it. So he did, but he didn't bring any money with him. "The nurse told me to come. That's why I'm here," he told Sharon when he presented himself for treatment. Mr. McCoy was no better. He promised he'd pay part of his bill after he saw the doctor, but when the time came, he turned out his pockets and rolled up his eyes. "Whatever happened to that twenty I had?" he mumbled. "Guess I'll have to pay you the first of the month."

The last time I saw her, Mrs. Carter was in bad shape. Her son had been stealing from her to buy drugs. Now the police were after him and her creditors were after her. It came as no surprise that her hypertension and diabetes were out of control. I referred her to Kathy, our counselor, and gave her two weeks worth of medication. "Don't worry about it now," I assured her. "Just pay us when you can."

Most distressing of all to the upstairs-me is our home care income. At Community Medical Care, home care is nurse-managed, with physician consultation as needed. Because we are not a home health agency, we receive no third-party reimbursement for home nursing visits and certainly not for "medical management" or chronic, long-term care. How do you charge elderly people on small, fixed incomes for services their insurance would cover if they were provided in our office, or in the

Nursing services are time-intensive. Nurses serve low-income populations. We specialize in outreach and follow-up. We are reluctant to compromise our standards of care.

home by a physician? Consider Bertha Killens. Ordinarily she is an office patient, but when an old foot ulcer opened up again, I hadn't the heart to make her hobble over to our office for dressing changes. She has Medicaid insurance that pays for office care and would, no doubt, have paid for a visiting nurse. But she's my patient and has been for years. I didn't refer. I saw her at home for free.

A home health agency wouldn't take on Euphoria Smith, even though she is homebound and has a Medicare card. She has diabetes, hypertension, arthritis, and is nearly blind, yet she manages alone. We have to adjust her medications occasionally and pre-fill her insulin syringes. We evaluate symptoms and soothe anxieties. We treat what we can and try to head off crises. She needs a nurse—and she has one, but we are not reimbursed over and above the $2 Mrs. Smith pays for each visit.

At the clinic, we live with the tension of an unbalanced budget and, although we don't get rich, we get by. But what about the nursing center we've been dreaming of for the neighborhood around Sixth and S Streets? Nursing services are time intensive. Nurses serve low-income populations. We specialize in outreach and follow-up. We are reluctant to compromise our standards of care. So how will this venture be financed? With the $2s and $5s and the occasional $20 that our clients can pay? Not likely. Certainly we're keeping our eyes on the nursing center demonstration projects recently funded by Congress, but wonder whether reimbursement will ever be available for the kind of care we give on the small scale on which we give it. Many economists and policymakers think such services will simply add to the already inflated costs of care without demonstrably improving health. I take some comfort in knowing that Mrs. Smith doesn't think so. For her, we're all there is.

Over the years, I assumed full management of the care of many of our patients. Despite my friendly reminders that I was a nurse, most of them simply decided that, as their doctor, I was entitled to call myself anything I wanted.

Years ago, when I first read it, I was swept up into Tom Wolfe's saga of the original Mercury astronauts, *The Right Stuff.* It was my introduction to the world of the test pilot, whose glamorous but risky profession is dedicated to "pushing the outside of the envelope." The envelope, Wolfe explained, is a "flight test term referring to the limits of a particular aircraft's performance, how tight a turn it could make at such-and-such a speed, and so on. 'Pushing the outside,' probing the outer limits, of the envelope seemed to be the great challenge and satisfaction of flight test."[6]

The book has helped me move toward a wider vision of nursing. Until quite recently, it was very important to me to remain unequivocally a nurse and to stay well within the confines of the nursing "envelope" as I conceived it. At one point during the early years at Community Medical Care, I actually plotted it out. I held myself responsible for a working knowledge of pathophysiology to this point, pharmacology to that point, behavioral science out to here, nutrition to there, and nursing theory way out yonder. Then, to continue the metaphor, I drew a line connecting the points. Inside the perimeter was what I called nursing. Inside there were challenges and satisfaction enough for me. And outside? I didn't view the vast expanse outside the "envelope" as uncharted, begging to be explored by enterprising nurses advancing the cause of health. I saw it as territory already staked out by other professions—social work, psychology, nutrition, health education and, most especially, medicine. I grew fond of categorical statements like "This is not a case for Veneta Masson" when confronted with problems or situations outside my realm.

Yet I had to admit that, as time went by, my practice was becoming less and less traditional. In fact, few of my patients (those I took care of at home being the exceptions) saw me as a nurse at all. Over the years, I had assumed full management of their health care in collaboration with Jim, CMC's physician. But despite that teamwork and my friendly reminders to patients that I was the nurse, most of them simply decided that, as their doctor, I was entitled to call myself anything I wanted.

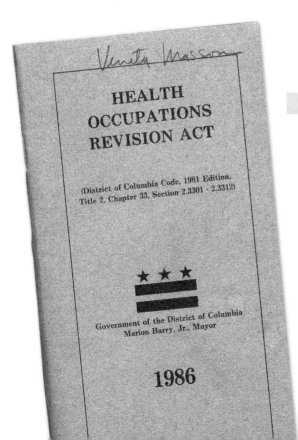

My mandate

Veneta Masson

HEALTH OCCUPATIONS REVISION ACT

(District of Columbia Code, 1981 Edition, Title 2, Chapter 33, Section 2.3301 - 2.3312)

★ ★ ★

Government of the District of Columbia
Marion Barry, Jr., Mayor

1986

One day, I overheard Sharon, the patient care coordinator, on the telephone explaining to someone that a particular patient was being referred to them by the nurse practitioner. It was my patient. "Wait," I said indignantly, "I am *not* a nurse practitioner."

"I know that," Sharon told me later, "but you have to learn to be flexible. People are beginning to understand what a nurse practitioner is and that's the only way I know to describe you."

For as many years as I had known about and associated professionally with nurse practitioners, I'd been uncertain whether they were inside or outside the envelope. In this, I had been influenced by nursing leaders like Martha Rogers, who said in a 1975 article that NPs were not nurses and, further, that "those nurses who leave nursing to be assistants to physicians under whatever title will soon find that their permission to practice anything will derive from… licensure under laws perpetrated by medicine for physician's assistants."[7] Lucille Kinlein, a nurse who established an independent practice dedicated to "caring with people" was just as adamant when she told some colleagues and me in 1980 that the practice of any nurse who works with any physician is, de facto, compromised.

I believed that becoming a nurse practitioner would mean forfeiting my independence, accepting the tyranny of protocols, formularies and other controls cunningly devised to hamper me in the full exercise of my nursing knowledge and skill.

My resistance finally crumbled in the face of a new District of Columbia nurse practice act that mandated separate credentialing for nurses in "advanced practice," and a professional liability insurance policy that, for the first time, required information regarding the applicant's scope of practice. I went back to school and became a nurse practitioner for no other purpose, I made a point of saying, than to keep on doing what I was already doing.

Surprise! I am still a nurse. A better nurse and a more effective healer. I've discovered that NPs are not outside the envelope but, like certain other groups and individuals within nursing, they are pushing the outside. From my new vantage point, I also see the uncharted expanse Out There where no other health profession is. I can go beyond what I know and what anyone else knows and just keep going as long as I have the ability—and the guts.

I look at the devastations caused by disease and poverty in the neighborhood around our clinic: AIDS, addictions of all kinds, children bearing children, children who have neither parenting nor homes, adults disabled while still in their prime, old people who are sick and alone. And I am firmly convinced that nurses are capable of finding solutions—maybe even cures—if we refuse to allow our imagination and forward movement to be thwarted by precedent, signs saying Do Not Enter, and restrictive notions about what nursing is.

According to the World Health Organization, primary
health care is the key to achieving an acceptable level
of health throughout the world. But it looked to me
as if health for all in the neighborhood surrounding
our clinic wouldn't happen any time soon.

What drew me to Community Medical Care in the first place was my interest in international health. Thirteen years ago, when CMC was just the germ of an idea gestating in Jim Hall's head, I was assuming new responsibilities as director of nursing for an international organization based in Washington, DC. Primary health care was coming into vogue. The 1978 Alma Ata conference on primary health care sponsored by the World Health Organization and the U.N. Children's Fund was on the horizon. "Health for All by the Year 2000" was a slogan I was beginning to hear at conferences and on trips to the developing world. "Primary health care is the key to achieving an acceptable level of health throughout the world in the foreseeable future...," I read in the literature and then quoted in my own project proposals. "It is equally valid for all countries, from the most to the least developed...."[8]

As I listened to Jim, a physician, talk with members of our church about starting a health "ministry" in a poor neighborhood in Washington, I heard phrases I might have put into my own program plans: essential health care, accessible and affordable, emphasizing education and health promotion, the full use of paraprofessionals and community involvement, enabling people to meet their own health needs. This sounds like the genuine article, I thought. Here's my chance to see how primary health care could work in my own city and country.

My curiosity piqued, I joined Jim's health task force as a participant-observer, but by the time we actually started giving health care, I was hooked. I found I needed more free time than I had, so I persuaded my employer to sponsor some of my expanded activities in this "domestic primary health care project." Within a few years I had left the field of international health to become CMC's nurse. Within six years I was also its director.

Now, with over a decade of firsthand experience, I sometimes find myself looking at what we have become in light of the guiding principles of the PHC movement. Take community involvement. Early on, we made contact with local leaders and groups. We invited patients and neighbors in to give us advice. We recruited community members for our board of directors. We even had a bona fide outreach worker for a time. But when you come right down to it, we are not a grassroots organization. We are three health professionals from outside the neighborhood who are equipped to provide a wide range of health services and three associates from inside the neighborhood with the savvy to tell us how to do it in a way we all hope is helpful and culturally acceptable.

And what about primary health care's emphasis on disease prevention and health promotion? Over the years we've tried to shift the focus from disease to health. We formed groups to help people lose weight, control diabetes, learn about contraception, and reduce stress. All were short-lived. "You don't put your business in the street," our patients told us, and we came to understand their reluctance to share personal information with people outside the family. So we tried individual health planning conferences — one patient with a team of staff members for an hour or more. "Too threatening," we were told. "And what's it for anyway?" We put on health fairs, special events, media presentations, you name it. What we discovered was that people in our community seem to respond best to health counseling when they're sick or scared, and then on a one-to-one basis. So what we try to provide is a mix of teaching and treatment.

Essential care, accessible and affordable? Those of our patients who have health insurance of one kind or another don't much care about our rock-bottom, sliding-scale fees, and many of those without insurance simply expect the system (us, in this case) to provide for them free of charge. Despite our protestations to the contrary, they firmly believe we get all the money we need from the government. As for what is essential, our idea is often at odds with our patients'. What's this? A physical with no blood tests, no X-ray? A consultation with no prescription at the end? What kind of place is this, anyway?

Are we accessible? Financially, yes. Physically, yes, except for those steps out in front of the building. But how can we be culturally accessible in an increasingly heterogeneous neighborhood when blacks and Hispanics eye each other with suspicion in the waiting room, elderly women shrink from the young adult males, and middle-class patients wonder about a place that caters to down-and-outs?

How do we measure up? Although I can name individuals and a few extended families who have received what I consider ideal primary health care, we have not even come close to effecting change in the community as a whole. It looks as if health for all at Ninth & P won't happen anytime soon. But Community Medical Care is there, a minor eccentricity in a galaxy of health institutions, providers, third-party payers, and policymakers that orbit around large, acute-care hospitals and their staff physicians—not around small, private, nonprofit primary health care centers.

PHOTO: JIM HALL

Jody consulting with Sharon

"Why, this place is just made for doing research," exclaimed a visiting colleague. "Have you got anything going?" Research? But I'm just a pragmatic practitioner, I thought to myself.

Every time it happens, I feel as if I've been stung. Like the time my colleague Mary, professor of nursing at a local university, came over to talk about using Community Medical Care as a clinical site for students. With one long look, she took in everything. Her eyes glittered. "Why, this place is just made for doing nursing research," she exclaimed. "Have you got anything going?"

"Well," I temporized, "I've got a number of ideas. It's just a matter of developing them." And I felt the sting, because I'd had those ideas for years and was no further toward forming them into research questions than on the day they'd occurred to me.

It happened again when I read Donna Diers's editorial on clinical scholarship in the spring 1988 *Image*. "We know you're out there," she wrote, "you nurses observing, thinking, trying to get better at the work. Thinking about how you do what you do and why and when, the choices in decisions and the choices in where you put your energies."[9]

Yes, I said to myself with conviction, here I am! I read on. "The repertoire of [the] clinical scholar is not just a collection of empirical observations," she explained, and proceeded to describe what it was, using terms like analysis, research, and writing it down. Oh, I thought, and felt the sting.

The sting is a mental twinge, a cognitive punctuation mark after every reminder that research is an integral part of nursing and that

I should be doing something about it. It's not that my practice never changes. I don't plod along year after year, according to protocol, looking neither to the right nor to the left, nor into a journal. Just ask me how to select a treatment for a particular stasis ulcer, or why adolescents start and stop using birth control pills, or how you might begin to wean a chronically ill elder from dependence on a market basket of drugs, or any one of a number of questions related to my work—I'll have plenty to tell you about what I've learned and how it has improved my effectiveness as a practitioner.

I draw on my own experience, that of my patients and colleagues, and the literature. How I synthesize all this may be scientific in the general sense of "producing knowledge," but I admit it's pretty soft stuff for a nurse who would fancy herself a clinical scholar. There is the drive to understand phenomena of concern to nursing and to help patients get better, but little in the way of focus, objectivity, and method.

Last year, in an effort to find out what shape clinical investigation might take in a setting like mine, I attended a two-day nursing research conference at a major university. While there, I met educators, graduate students, and a sprinkling of clinical specialists, but no one else whose bread and butter was hands-on nursing practice. About sixty papers were presented, only one-third of them with potential for clinical application and a handful with any relevance to my field, primary health care. Although time was allotted for group discussion, there were no formal critiques by peers. The only thing I brought home to CMC was some practical information on the disposal of sharps from a poster session.

I rationalized my disappointment with the thought that, after all, one conference can hardly be representative of the whole field of nursing research. So I went to the library to consult the journals. In my carrel, I started through the tables of contents, abstracts, and article after article reporting on nurses' attitudes toward…, patients' perceptions of…, X's theory applied to…, factors that influence…, and relationships among…. There was no instant gratification for the pragmatic practitioner.

I confess that when the flier for my Sigma Theta Tau chapter's annual research meeting arrived and I saw that the featured papers were, in order, "The Influence of…," "The Relationship of…," and "Perceptions of. . . ," I could not muster enough enthusiasm to go. I confess further that I am still sitting on the most recent solicitation from the American Nurses' Foundation, knowing that it needs my support but wanting a greater return on my investment than I suspect I'll receive.

It's not that I don't believe studies of nurses, nursing systems, and the profession of nursing (as opposed to nursing care) have their place. And I realize that, even in clinical research, clinical applications are often apparent only after the foundation of the research pyramid has been laid brick by brick, small study by small study. I know there is exciting work going on out there. I always look for the capsule summaries of research reports in the practice-oriented publications that include them. And I read everything Patricia Benner writes on the knowledge that is embedded in clinical practice.

But as a would-be clinical scholar, I find it hard to distance myself mentally and physically from the specific needs of individual patients. I have the inevitable constraints on my time and scope of practice. There is a lot I don't know about how to find answers to the questions that lurk in the depths of my mind. Like most of us, I opt for the quick fix. Yet, despite it all, even as I write this, I feel the sting.

When I read Virginia Woolf's book for the first time, I had just begun to experience what financial security, leisure, and a room of my own could mean for my professional growth.

Virginia Woolf was not thinking about nurses but about women and fiction when she issued her prescription in 1928. It applies to nurses just the same. It is this: "A woman must have money and a room of her own if she is to write fiction."[10] Money—that is, a secure income—can buy one the leisure to contemplate; a room of one's own stood for the power to think for oneself. Without these, she believed, the full creative potential of women writers and, indeed, of women in general, would be unrealized.

When I read her essay for the first time, I had just begun to experience what financial security (in my case, the economic subsidy of marriage), leisure, and a room of my own could mean for my professional growth. In 1980, I cut the thinning cord that tied me to a position with an attractive salary, opportunities for advancement, and a modest place on the national nursing scene to throw in my lot with the little group at Community Medical Care, the clinic I had helped to found in 1978. In those early days, CMC could not provide me with a full-time job or a living wage. I decided to forfeit both and see what came. It wasn't easy. The surplus time I planned to use for personal and professional enrichment hung heavily. And, despite the fact that I did not need a higher salary than CMC could pay, I was ruffled by lighthearted remarks from colleagues bent on climbing the ladder of success: "So when are you going to get a real job?" one asked. "You are what you earn, you know," warned another.

I brooded. To discipline myself and provide some structure, I began to keep a journal of life at the clinic. I'd sit in my study and write about my coworkers, my patients, and the results of my efforts on their behalf. I also wrote about books and periodicals I'd read, people I'd met, conferences I'd attended, my intermittent hankering for the fast-paced life I'd left behind, and my preoccupation with my prospects as a novice practitioner in primary health care. Gradually what I wrote began to instruct me. Ideas would flit through my head like fireflies. I'd catch them, play with them, and painstakingly pin them down with words on paper so that I could come back and examine them later.

An early journal entry starts, "Let's face it. Sometimes I feel like I'm trapped in a small room with a low ceiling." Measuring myself against Jim, the physician, I felt diminished by my role as nurse. There were no other health care providers at CMC at the time, just him and me in a kind of unrelenting professional intimacy. Why, I asked myself, couldn't I do what he did, in the way he did it and at the same speed?

One of the great discoveries of my life came while I was reading Irene Claremont de Castillejo's *Knowing Woman*.[11] The door to some unexplored passageway in my mind flew open and I began to see clearly for the first time just what nursing is. (Years later, I'm amused, even embarrassed, to see my excitement splattered all over my journal pages of April 1980.) I started recording anecdotes that showed how Jim and I made music together, not in unison, but in an intricate counterpoint that seemed to embrace and heal patients. I began to appraise myself differently, to speak in my own voice, follow my instincts, move at my own pace. A December entry marked my progress that year: "I want to turn my looking glass into a window on the world." Having experienced a fundamental shift in perspective, I was ready to look at the larger world of nursing in terms of what I was learning in my small one.

Over the years, held accountable by a church community that values centeredness, quiet contemplation, the exercise of one's gifts, and following one's calling, I have continued, in spite of a busier schedule, to spend time in this room of my own. It's where I withdraw to puzzle out problems, entertain possibilities, and let my thoughts run free.

I think sometimes of Florence Nightingale and wonder if she could have achieved what she did politically and professionally without the £500 a year "settled upon her" by her father when she was thirty-three and the privacy and intellectual freedom afforded by a place of her own in London which, at the height of her powers, she never left. Most of us are not mental giants with powerful connections and independent means. We may find no time in our workday to eat, much less to think. Our career decisions may be dictated by financial and family considerations. We may choose to keep our free time just that: free.

But what would happen if those of us with the personal resources, and the yen to do so, regularly sought a quiet place for creative reflection on the challenges that confront us as individual practitioners and as members of a large, diverse and action-oriented occupational group? Virginia Woolf writes that "it is in our idleness, in our dreams, that the submerged truth sometimes comes to the top." I, too, have found that the clarity that so often eludes me in the hurly-burly of patients and paperwork and everyday crises has a way of shining through when I sit here in my room, idly watching for fireflies.

A recent nursing school graduate I know wants to make her career in community nursing but has been told she should work a year in the hospital first. Is it true? she asks. I reply.

That final conference is still fresh in my mind. It is my last nursing course. I am completing my summer practicum in the hospital where I have learned most of what I know about clinical nursing. My instructor and I are in an office adjacent to the nurses' station. She asks me, as she has asked the others, "What have you decided to do after you graduate?" I do not hesitate. I tell her that I have decided to stay on at the hospital and work a year on a medical-surgical unit. She nods approval. I have given the preferred answer. I already know that I want to go on to school and then into public health, but the importance of that year of hospital nursing has been ingrained in me and I accept it as I accept everything else I have been taught about nursing. I do my year. It is a good experience that I draw on repeatedly in years to come. Convinced that the advice is sound, I begin to pass it on to nursing students and new graduates who come to me to talk about their future.

The last time this happened was a month ago — twenty-odd years after my own graduation. "I have an interview for a position in the health department," the recent graduate said. "It's a position in maternal child health — the kind of job I've always wanted. There's only one problem. I haven't had much hospital experience yet. I've always been told you need at least a year. Do you think the health department will be interested in hiring me without it? And what if I want to go back to hospital nursing later? Will I have lost all my skills? Will they hire me back?"

COMPLETE YOUR EDUCATION
THEN COME WITH ME
I LEAD TO WORLD WIDE OPPORTUNITY.

Note card featuring
American Red Cross
nurse recruitment
poster, circa 1915
(see page 205)

"What a coincidence that you should ask," I said. "A group of us were discussing this very thing just the other day." And so we had. All of us worked in community settings, although at least two had feet in both worlds, community and hospital. In a spirit of bemused resignation, we analyzed the rationale for The Year. Skill reinforcement was the major part of it, we agreed. At graduation, one's grasp of the motor skills basic to nursing is still tenuous, as is the ability to orchestrate a full complement of nursing activities to the rhythm of the various shifts into which the hospital day is divided.

But there is more to the rationale than that, we decided. Since hospitals have been the primary place of employment for recent generations of nurses and represent the one experience we all hold in common, it has become the standard by which we judge each other and are judged in turn. One by one, those of us sitting around the table recalled recent visits to hospitals during which we had wondered how we would fare if unexpectedly called to take over some nursing function that had to do with the operation of equipment that we had never seen before or knew about in theory only. Could we do it? Would we have the right stuff? Were we still "good nurses"?

We concluded that we were asking ourselves the wrong questions. The pertinent question is, "Does the rationale for The Year still hold?" While the hospital is still the workshop in which lay people learn to be nurses, it may not remain their primary place of employment. Until recently, 75 percent of all employed nurses worked in hospitals. The current figure is about 60 percent.[12,13] With the evolution of new technologies, hospital nurses are becoming increasingly specialized. The question of what constitutes basic skills is moot. Is there a package of basic skills that can carry a nurse from maternity to neurology? From neonatology to gerontology? From acute care to primary care? From hospital to community? From 1980 to 1990? The answer is no. The rest of the answer is continuing education. This is what I told my younger colleague. But I did not stop there.

Have you ever thought what would happen to hospitals if new graduates went to the community first? Perhaps that is the question we should be asking ourselves as a profession. Without doubt, hospitals are a world apart. For a nurse whose only experience is in the hospital, the larger world of health care is hard to envision. How can you think in terms of wellness when you see only sick people? How can you look at patients holistically when you do not have a clear idea where they came from, who they were before they got sick, and what is likely to become of them after they leave the hospital?

How can you actively involve a patient in his own care when someone else hands him his medications and prepares his meals? when staff members rather than family members or friends—or no one— assists with daily care? How can you learn to be fully accountable for your actions and confident in making decisions when you seldom have opportunities to work on your own in an uncontrolled environment?

How can you judge the long-term effects of treatment, teaching and discharge planning when you have to say goodbye to your patient at the door of the hospital?

How can you get a perspective on what the shrinking health care dollar will buy when you still have the luxury of saying that the patient's needs come first? when you run through countless disposables every day? when you schedule any diagnostic or therapeutic procedure that might be relevant to the patient's condition? when you do not have to help patients understand their itemized hospital bill in terms of what their insurance will cover or in relation to charges for comparable items or services outside the hospital?

I may have been exceptionally naive as a new graduate working in the hospital, but I still remember my surprise when I got into patients' homes and found that they do not always fill their prescriptions or take the ones they have filled; that most people on special diets do not follow them for very long after discharge; that many clean people do not bathe every day—or at least between 8 AM and 12 noon; that patients often do not know their physicians prior to hospitalization or understand a fraction of what has been done to them during their hospital stay (including what kind of surgery they had); that discharge plans frequently fall through; that health is not necessarily a priority when weighed against children's school expenses, auto repairs, convenience foods, or "the way I've always done things."

I would be a very different hospital nurse coming back from the community now, and more effective, I believe, even though I would have to learn or relearn many technical skills. I would bring to the hospital a broader perspective on health care, an understanding of health in the hierarchy of values, experience with family systems and community politics and how things get done or don't—and why. It would not be easy to adapt to changing shifts or the confinement of intramural life, but I would see familiar routines, policies, and situations with new eyes, sharpened organizational skills, and some useful ideas about how to adapt nursing care to a changing economic and social climate.

We are facing a new nurse shortage, one that is aggravated by shrinking enrollments in nursing schools and closures of schools that are too expensive to maintain without a steady flow of federal funds. In her thoughtful analysis of the shortage, Patricia Moccia said that change in the relationship of nursing with the health care system and the larger society is needed to resolve nursing crises and that "instead of using energies and resources to recruit and retain students in the system as it is designed now, we might commit ourselves to changing the health care system....[14]

In another editorial on the same theme, Maryann Fralic suggested that we adopt the "what if?" approach to solving our problems— leave the traditional wisdom behind and let imagination run free.[15] So, what if new graduates were encouraged to work in the community first to learn skills that could be brought back into institutions? Home health agencies are busy recruiting hospital nurses with acute care skills to take care of patients discharged quicker and sicker. What if hospitals went out looking for seasoned community nurses to address the needs of those inside? It might offer an intriguing opportunity for reform from outside the hospital but from inside the profession.

What makes a good nurse? My patient, Winnie, had no trouble telling me. So why do I persist in trying to judge nurses according to their education and credentials rather than their mastery of the healing art?

What makes a good nurse? I don't recall ever asking the question in so many words, so I was surprised when I realized I had an answer in mind. It surfaced when I went to the hospital to visit Winnie Smead, a longtime patient at Community Medical Care, now hospitalized with cancer. On past visits she had told me about the nurses on her unit and what went on as they attended patients or talked among themselves in the corridors. Whenever Winnie described something a good nurse had done, I smiled a "but of course we're wonderful" smile.

This day it was different. She frowned as she described a personal encounter with a "bad" nurse and had little difficulty convincing me that she had experienced poor, if not outright bad, nursing. The first thing I heard myself say in response was "Do you know if it was a registered nurse?" She said she was not sure. I sat wondering, was it a nursing assistant, a practical nurse, or a registered nurse? (I knew I could trust Winnie to tell a nurse from a non-nurse.) Then she caught my attention with a wave of the hand. "Wait," she said. "Now I remember. She had RN after her name." Now I badly wanted to know whether the nurse had a two-year associate degree, a three-year diploma, a bachelor's or, possibly, master's degree. She could not, of course, tell me. "What difference does it make," she said. It was a statement, not a question.

It came to me that I expected the quality of nursing care, from poorest to best, to correspond to the nurse's level of formal education, from least to most. And, by extension, I must have thought that if all caregivers were RNs—and all RNs were college graduates—patients would be better nursed. As I left Winnie's room and walked past the nurses' station lost in thought, I asked myself how such a thing could be true. After all, even I could not tell which of Winnie's nurses had what credentials just by watching them at work. I could only tell the good ones from the poor ones, and my rating was generally the same as Winnie's. Since that day, I have thought a lot about what makes a good nurse.

Take my colleague Judy and me. We both do primary health care in small clinics. Judy has a diploma as a basis for her nurse practitioner training. I have a master's degree as a basis for mine. Am I, therefore, a better nurse than Judy? No. To be perfectly honest, I sometimes wonder how I measure up to someone like Mrs. Gideon, the wife of one of my patients who, with no formal training, has nursed her completely incapacitated husband twenty-four hours a day, both in the hospital and at home, for over ten years. While in her care, he has never had a bedsore, or pneumonia, or any new symptom for which she did not take appropriate action.

Unlike Mrs. Gideon's, my own entry into practice was formal. As a hospital volunteer, I learned to be at ease in the presence of sick people and to care for them in simple ways. As an associate degree student, I acquired a basic understanding of illness and learned to use the fundamental nursing skills to nurse persons with various diseases and disabilities. As a student in a baccalaureate program, I improved my communication skills and was introduced to nursing outside the hospital while expanding my general knowledge of the social sciences and humanities. As a master's student in community health nursing, I studied public health, epidemiology, nursing theory, research, and teaching—but had little contact with patients. As a post-master's student in a nurse practitioner program, I learned a great deal about pathophysiology, pharmacology, and clinical medicine—but nothing new about nursing. I sometimes wonder what would have happened had I not returned to school after finishing my associate degree. Would I be a less effective nurse, or a better one? After all, I would have twenty-six years of experience by now, uninterrupted by breaks for continued education and jobs that took me away from hands-on nursing.

It is a moot point. But the question of what makes a good nurse deserves an answer. Here is mine: Unlike medicine, which is a body of knowledge with applications for the diagnosis and treatment of disease, nursing is first and foremost an act, a process. Not the problem solving process translated into nursing jargon, but the process of healing through care and nurture. You don't learn it from lectures or books as well as you learn it by watching, listening, and doing. It is performance art. Like dancing. Like playing a musical instrument. That is why I can call Mrs. Gideon a good nurse. Not only did she follow her own nurturing

PHOTO: JIM HALL

Winnie and me at her house

instincts, perfecting her skills through trial and error, she also learned by watching and working alongside her husband's hospital and home care nurses. She has had a long and arduous preceptorship. Instead of a diploma, she has one well-nursed patient as testimony to her skill.

My experience was not so different. Most of what I know about hospital nursing I learned my first year in practice from Ruby Wright, an LPN, and Reiko Hatakeda, an RN. What I know about nursing in the community I learned as I went along from my own experience and my colleagues.

So why do I persist in trying to judge nurses according to their education and credentials and not according to their mastery of the healing art? I have to admit to a lingering expectation that there is some straightforward way to achieve and measure nursing expertise. And I want to believe that all the years I spent in classrooms and libraries have made me a good nurse. They have certainly made me a more astute diagnostician and a better technician. They have equipped me to work in certain settings and capacities. They have given me a deeper understanding of human nature and contributed to my intellectual maturity. But if I am a good nurse, I believe I owe it to practice and to informal learning from other nurses at all "levels." They and my patients are the only ones who can grant me that prized credential.

My friend and colleague, Teresa, is a good nurse, my nurse. She says she began this poem on Friday evening of a long, stressful week. The impulse for it came from a song we sometimes sang together called "Here I Am, Lord" by Dan Schutt, a song based on these words from the prophet Isaiah:

Then I heard the Lord saying,
   Whom shall I send?
  Who will go for us?
     And I answered, Here am I; send me.
        Isaiah 6:8

Here I am, Lord,
    sitting face to face with Ms. Benson.
    She's confused, they say,
    walks the neighborhood—
    can't find her way back.
    Her wig is on backward.
    She hears echos when I talk.
    All her tests are negative
        but what's going on?

Here I am, Lord,
    sitting face to face with a neurologist.
    Not for me, mind you,
    but for Ms. Benson.
    For six weeks I've tried to arrange

a consultation to evaluate her memory loss
and then called her last night
to remind her I'd pick her up at eight.
I arrived
    knocked on the door
        no answer
so here I am alone
with the neurologist.

Here I am, Lord,
    standing outside Ms. Hammond's
    burning apartment building.
    Ms. Hammond is ninety-eight
      walks with the aid of a shopping cart
        and is homebound for a year.
As I clip her nails,
the curtains across the hallway catch fire.
The hallway is black with smoke
and tenants are screaming.
I carry Ms. Hammond
with the help of two others.
Gasping for air
we arrive outdoors.
I'm grateful to be alive
but Ms. Hammond has other things
    on her mind.
She turns to me and asks,
    "While I'm out,
      could you bring me to the drugstore
        to buy some hair salve?"

Here I am, Lord,
  holding a newborn baby boy
  in my arms.
  His mom and dad are parents
  for the first time.
  I did the urine test that
  confirmed the pregnancy.
  I listened to his mom
  throughout the pregnancy
  share the story of her abuse
  as a child.
  "I'm scared," she said.
  "Don't want to ever hurt my baby."
  She holds him close,
      keeps him warm.
              "Thanks for being here," she says.

Here I am, Lord,
  doing a school physical
  for five-year-old DeWayne.
  I open his chart
  to record his school-age immunizations
  and realize I have given him
  every immunization
  since he was two months old.
      Where has the time gone?

Here I am, Lord,
    reflecting on the last year,
    remembering the bizarre
    as well as the blessings,
    remembering the moments I ask
        Why am I here?
    to the moments I am grateful that
        Here I am, Lord.
        I will go, Lord, if you lead me.
                But for now
                in this time
                in this place
                I will hold your people
                in my heart.

I am a nurse. I work for good. I commit no political
acts... do I?

It was after we examined the Hispanic woman whose complaint was itch-
ing and discomfort in a keloid at the site of a breast biopsy that Eduardo
showed me some of his: shiny red burrows, two, three centimeters long,
studding his chest like crude tribal markings. "Yes, they itch sometimes,"
he said, "but there is nothing you can do." That Monday afternoon last
summer, the day we saw the lady with the keloid, was the day Eduardo
began to tell me his story. I'd heard parts of it from others long before he
began volunteering his Mondays at Community Medical Care. Hearing
it now from him, in his own language, in snatched moments
on a succession of Mondays, I am finally beginning to understand it.

Eduardo is forty, a physician, and married with two children. For the
past five years he has lived in the Washington suburbs. Before that, he
spent time in Mexico, en route from his own country, El Salvador. He left
El Salvador after his release from prison. The imprisonment was only a
matter of days, he points out, owing to the fact that the son of a woman
who used to sell produce to his mother happened to be well placed
in the police department and able to help him. But, he adds, a lot can
happen in a short time.

Why was he arrested? He had become interested in working with the
poor in a neighborhood not far from his boyhood home. Because he
realized that their needs extended beyond the health care he was able to
provide, he also taught in a literacy training program and, because life is
not all work, began to participate in the social life of the community.

One night, some friends, members of a local labor union, arrived at
his door with a young man who had been shot. They couldn't take him to
the hospital, they said, because the police were looking for him. Eduardo

did what he could for the wounded man and the group went its way. Sometime later, the police came for Eduardo. They took him to the station for interrogation. As they questioned him about the young man and Eduardo's union friends, they smoked. And after each smoke, one of them would lean forward and stub out the cigarette on Eduardo's chest. That was not the worst of it, but it marked him forever. "When I take my children swimming, people stare at me," he says, smiling. "I think they think I have a skin disease." At the lake on the day of our staff picnic, I noticed that Eduardo wore his T-shirt into the water.

Months passed since my talks with Eduardo began. Then I had a thought I'd never had before. Where it came from I don't know, nor what triggered it. I only know that it seared through my brain like a bullet.

It was lunchtime. Eduardo and I were sitting upstairs in the clinic, chatting. He was sipping a Coke. I was peeling an orange. "Eduardo," I asked abruptly, "if this clinic, our little clinic on Ninth Street, were in El Salvador and we were going about our business, just as we are today, would we be considered subversive?" He stopped sipping and looked at me. He nodded his head yes.

Of course we would. We serve the poor. We are affiliated with a church. In addition to giving health care, we sometimes help people get what they are entitled to from the government. It's called advocacy. The Central Americans we see are the same ones Eduardo took care of in El Salvador. And many of our other patients live outside the law.

But *I* am not subversive. Beyond voting, I commit no political acts. I am not even an idealist. I helped to start the clinic because I had a professional interest in primary health care. When I joined Amnesty International, it was in a fit of pique over the ticket I got for disobeying a traffic sign hidden behind a billboard. If this can happen to me on a street in Washington, DC, I reasoned, think what could happen in a country where there is no protection or recourse under the law!

But is a country like El Salvador really so alien? I have visited there more than once. No, not on a peace mission or fact-finding tour, but accompanying my husband on business trips. What impressed me most each time was the apparent normalcy of daily life. In spite of the fact that this was a country at war with itself, the people I met went to work every day, ate oranges, and drank Coke. Yes, I saw desperately poor people, just like I do in Washington. Sure, the army was everywhere, but so are the police on Ninth Street. When I learned about a resolution put before the American Nurses Association to protest attacks on Salvadoran nurses working in outlying clinics and hospitals, I felt that American nurses were being given an unbalanced picture of the risks health workers there faced. If nurses disappeared, shouldn't we at least consider the possibility that they were doing more than nursing?

Today, I feel differently. Today, I can imagine myself in a situation where simple advocacy of health care for all could be viewed as a threat to the stability of a political system: I am at the clinic, going about my business, when a man stalks in, flashes a badge and says he wants to speak with me. "What can I do for you?" I ask, taking him into an exam room and shutting the door. "I think you're aware," he says, with no attempt to hide his sarcasm, "that there's a war on law and order in this neighborhood. Mighty dangerous place for folks like you to be working. I'm sure you would claim not to know it, but a few hours ago, a man was seen leaving this clinic—a man suspected of shooting one of our agents two blocks from here yesterday. He got hurt, too, but never showed up in any of the local emergency rooms. Don't you find that interesting?" He pauses, gives me a significant look. "Now, here's my advice," he says. "Move your clinic out of this neighborhood before something bad happens to you. I guarantee that if you stay here, you'll regret it."

What would I do? Would I choose to get his meaning? Would I throw away my investment in this place? Turn my back on these people who may have started out as patients but who have become friends and, some of them, coworkers? I am a nurse. I work for good. I commit no political acts…do I?

This could have been the story of any number of the Central American women who were moving into the clinic neighborhood and seeking out "la doctora Veneta."

Like the others, she is not from here
and when she came she left
all of what matters behind —
four children, a village
a father (not well), the lingering
scent of her man (who had fled)
Sunday walks in the plaza after mass
on days when the soldiers were gone
on days when no bodies were found.

The journey from home was perilous —
sometimes on foot, or crowded
into the back of a truck, over hills
through dense forests, arroyos
dark rivers, toward menacing lights,
the eyes of hostile cities.

The trip cost her more than
she wanted to pay —
all the crumpled bills
from the earthenware jar
in the wall of the house,
the silver bracelets and earrings
passed down from her mother.
Her body they took along the way

again and again as if for a debt
that can never be paid.
What drove her on was a woman's
fixed and singular faith that
she is the giver of life
the mother of God.

By bus from the border
by phone from the station
by foot to the room of the friend
of a cousin who knew of a place
and jobs cleaning offices at night
where no questions were asked
and dollars were paid
unless you missed work
or were caught by the migra—
all this distance she came
numb to the pain in her feet and back
and the ache in her lower heart.

She spent her days trying to sleep.
Nights she roamed large empty halls
as wide as the streets
that gave onto the plaza
pushing a cart full of cleaning supplies
bagging the trash, sweeping the floors
washing away the stains of another
day in the upper world.
Paydays she sent her money home
by the man at Urgente Express.
Sunday she sometimes walked
down the street at the edge

of the park, watching
with shaded eyes among the men
for one she might know.

Months passed this way
and with each one she wept
the tears of blood that women weep
and felt the ache in her belly
grow stronger until at last
there was no relief,
come new moon or full,
and no poultice, tea or prayer
that helped her bear
what she must bear.

She sits in the clinic —
"a 32-year-old Hispanic female
complaining of chronic pelvic pain."

The results of all the tests
are negative, they say.
That means there's nothing we can find
to blame for all the pain.
There is a cause, of course —
perhaps a scar deep inside.
Surgery might tell us more — or not,
but then there's the matter of money.

I see, she says simply.
*Well, if you can't find
anything wrong — and you know
there is no money…*

There are some pills
you could take, they say,
for the pain, when it
bothers you most.

You are kind, she says
and stands up to go,
like the others,
from here to her job,
her room, and perhaps twice a year
to a telephone that spans the miles
of dense forest, dark river
to the house of a friend
of an aunt of her father
to ask if the children
are well and in school
on days when the soldiers are gone
on days when no bodies are found.

*I will send for them
one day soon*, she says.
For now there is only the ache in her belly,
come new moon or full,
and no poultice, pill or prayer
to help her bear
what she must bear.

What drives her on is a woman's
fixed and singular faith that
she is the giver of life
the mother of God.

DRAWING: KATHY BRUNKOW

At the clinic, we have off days. But to give credit
where it is due, we pay attention to the spirit of the
place. What our knowledge and skill can't cure, we hope
this can. Like Jim, Sharon, Teresa, and me, Dorothy,
once a teenage patient and now CMC's medical assistant,
has become very much a part of this place.

On busy days at Community Medical Care, small talk among staff members gets saved up for the end: that half hour or so after the front door is locked and the "Closed" sign flips down. It's then that we tie up loose ends, exchange messages, and make some effort to set the place to rights for tomorrow. This day Sharon, cradling the telephone between ear and shoulder, on hold for the pharmacist, wants to tell me what Charlotte Smith, a new patient, said about us. I turn off the vacuum cleaner so I can hear. "She said, 'This place seems more like a home than a clinic.' I told her I guessed she was right."

I bend over to pick up a stray toy from behind a potted plant as I think about how to react. Sharon is impatient and prompts me: "That's good, silly. She meant it as a compliment."

"I know it," I say, and I do. In fact, CMC has become more home than home for a number of us, including some patients, especially those who have been displaced to other parts of the city as gentrification of this poor neighborhood advances. They live in the projects in Southeast Washington now, but Shaw is home and they continue to come here by bus to do their business and spend their days.

I think for a moment about what Charlotte Smith would have seen when she came for her appointment this afternoon. She wouldn't have missed Kevin, Sharon's happy one-year-old, sitting under the front desk, rubbing peanut butter-cheese crackers into the rug, or Dorothy's birthday balloon floating around the waiting room and down the hall like the Goodyear blimp. Everyone notices Rhosu's African-American abstract, hung in the place of honor over the small, often overlooked sign requesting payment at the time service is rendered. Then there was Mr. Funt, in the flesh, asleep in one of the Bank of England chairs I was so proud of until each of the four G. children carved their initials into the wood while waiting for their well child visits one fine morning. The building itself is beyond apology—but it matches the others on the block. And our housekeeping varies between compulsive and laissez-faire, reflecting the personalities of the staff members responsible for cleaning up on a given day.

I consider what Charlotte Smith might have heard this afternoon. Not, I hope, the words between Jim and Sharon about the page that was never answered, or Paula's sobs as she confessed to Sharon that she'd beaten her hyperactive son, Roger, again. She couldn't have missed the banging on the pipes from the third floor where they are renovating. But she might have paid more attention to the black gospel tapes we were playing until the Arias family arrived and Dorothy switched over to Salvadoran music. I know for a fact she was one of the patients engaged in a hot discussion about whether or not the Mayor should resign, because I, too, was lured out to the waiting room for several minutes when I should have been charting.

In the end, it is the spirit of place that I am most concerned about. What did Charlotte Smith feel when she walked in the door—and as she walked out again? Did she feel better? If so, did the place itself contribute to her sense of well-being? My personal interest in creating environments in which healing can happen must have started as instinct. I hadn't yet read Nightingale's *Notes on Nursing*, that mother lode of nursing lore, but I seem always to have known that there were places that emanated healing and places that did not. I remember hospital rooms and wards that I believe contributed to a patient's recovery and others that did not. The physical surroundings were important, to be sure, but there was also the atmosphere created by the staff as they cared for patients and interacted with each other. It is the same outside the hospital. When I make home visits, my antenna is always up to receive signals from the environment. Frequently, I find I have to devote as much attention to cleaning, creating order, and attending to the needs of others in the house as I do to the person who is my patient if that person is going to get better.

It is as true today as it was when Nightingale wrote, that "the exact value of particular remedies and modes of treatment is by no means ascertained, while there is universal experience as to the extreme importance of careful nursing in determining the [outcome of] the disease."[16] For me, at Community Medical Care, that includes nursing the staff and the place as well as the patients.

The other day Teresa, who has a faculty appointment in one of the local nursing schools, came back to the clinic after supervising students in the outpatient department of a large teaching hospital that serves the same population we do. She was disturbed by the noise, the blank walls, the long lines of chairs occupied by mothers and infants waiting hour after hour for clinic appointments. "Just being there gave me a headache," she said. "All I wanted when I left was fifteen minutes of peace and quiet." I wonder about a place, ostensibly a house of healing that can give a healthy person a headache. What might it do to a sick person confined inside for days or weeks at a time?

At CMC, we have off days. But to give credit where it is due, we pay attention to the spirit of the place. What our knowledge and skill can't cure, we hope this can. We think about what makes us feel at home as well as what will feel welcoming and familiar to people in the neighborhood. We tend to our life together, too, with weekly "family time," celebrations whenever we can find an excuse, even getaways.

Listen a while and you'll hear discordant notes as ordinary and extraordinary stressors play on the idiosyncracies and weaknesses of each of us. But these have not succeeded in marring the basic harmony that results from our positive regard for each other, our shared history, and our vocation as healers. Funny. When Mr. Funt woke up after his nap he thanked everyone and left, forgetting the fact that he hadn't yet been seen. When Sharon reminded him, he said that was all right, he felt fine now. He went out the door humming.

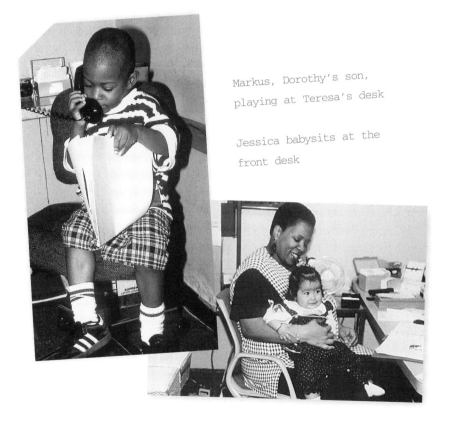

Markus, Dorothy's son, playing at Teresa's desk

Jessica babysits at the front desk

I'd be less than honest if I didn't admit to a mix
of emotions on days like this one.

It was a $5 day.
That's all I could say
to a person who thinks
a clinic like ours
surely gets its share
of the millions this country
spends on health care.

That's what our landlord thinks
when he raises the rent
and tells us he's pleased
to help us serve the community.
That's what the plumber thinks
as he works on the downstairs
toilet again and charges us more
than we charged him for a visit.

That's what salesmen think
when they call about high-tech
solutions and get-rich schemes,
and what Trudy thinks
every time she pockets
the Phisoderm soap on the sink
or loses the pills we give her.

But I know different.
At day's end when we lock up
the clinic and do the count
of patients and money, and hide
the day's take in the lockbox
under the desk in the lab
I know different.

Sharon and I look at
the names of the twenty-odd
patients we saw today—
some new, some we know
some young, some old
some here, some at home.
We see what we did
and how much they paid
or didn't.

There's Tony who's three
and not talking yet,
Ms. Giles who can't stoop
to do day's work because of
the nagging pain in her back,
a nervous young man who gave
two names and thought he had
a social disease.

Clarence's stomach was burning
like fire — he's the first to admit
he's back on booze,
and Bonnie's desperate
to stop smoking crack
for fear of losing her job
at the school.

Tonya cried when she heard
she was pregnant. She can't
support another child.
Maria was here, cradling
the fruit of her fortieth year,
a newborn boy,
and she'd been convinced
she could never conceive!

Two elderly ladies
got checked-up for church camp
and Sateen Clark got
shots for school.
Miss Bea who has sugar
and too much cholesterol
turns eighty tomorrow
in spite of it all.

Lula Hill we saw at home
to treat the ulcer
on her foot, and we made
a stop at Mr. Ward's
when his wife phoned to say
he'd had another one
of his spells.

Trudy arrived, to no one's
surprise, and lay spread-eagled
on the floor by way of getting
attention. Poor Verla Mae
nearly suffered a stroke
when she opened the door
and saw her. Well, my pressure's
gonna be up today, she warned.

These and others came
and went, but no one came
with money. Not one check
arrived in the mail,
only a past due utility bill.
The forty dollars we use
to make change was all we had
and we'd started with that
in the morning.

It's after six.
There's a knock at the door.
Let's not answer it, I say.
It can only mean trouble
this time of day.
Maybe it's Trudy, back
for more soap or pills.
I go anyway.

It's Tom, Ms. Carter's
oldest boy. My mother sent me
to give you this. She wants
to pay something on her bill.
She said for me to say thanks.
Thanks.
He's gone like a shot.

I close the door
open the envelope and count
the five crumpled $1s inside.
Hmmm, says Sharon
writing it down,
I thought today would
add up to nothing
but now it's a $5 day.

If you didn't chart it, you didn't do it, runs the grave old adage. But there is plenty I do in any patient encounter that never makes it into words much less onto paper. This is not petty stuff either. It is at the heart of my work.

Call me compulsive. Sharon, our clinic's patient care coordinator, does. She stands beside my desk, watching the process unfold yet again. I sit hunched over a patient's chart weeding out the thicket of staples that have tacked page after page of white carrier sheets to the right-hand side of the folder and green summary sheets to the left side. After adding new sheets and pulling out unnecessary items — correspondence from third-party payers, old notes from one staff member to another, reminders — I staple the chart back together again: two staples top right and two top left. Next I paste any loose lab reports or medical record forms onto a carrier sheet. Children's charts get an orange sticker; home care patients, a green one.

If the chart still looks shabby, I may decide to scrap the folder and start over with a fresh one. Only then do I begin to sift through the contents to update the problem list, long-term medication list, encounter log, and preventive health screening record. Sometimes I trace a specific problem back through time. Occasionally I want to take notes for a written summary of the entire record. As I sit back to admire my handiwork, Sharon, if she has been able to restrain herself until now, will point out how much time this little project has consumed and whether the next patient has been inconvenienced by my dalliance with a pile of papers.

Please don't misunderstand. I do my share of griping about paper-work. I would rather spend time with patients than with their charts. I don't like knowing that someone is waiting to see me while I am still writing about the last person. And I don't like facing another half-hour of charting after office hours are over. It's not that I am logopho-bic, to answer the question Judith Hays asked in her article on the documentation of nursing care.[17] I have to admit that I enjoy the chal-lenge of representing a patient's language, harmonizing it with my own, then translating it into therapeutic, fiscal, or legal vocabulary as prescribed by the institutions that govern health care today. And I like precise language. The other day I left a SOAP note (that wonderful acronym for the Subjective and Objective medical history and the clinician's Assessment and Plan) in the middle of the "O" until I could locate the term for the part of the outer ear just inside the rim: antihelix. Ah!

Maybe my preoccupation with charts comes from taking to heart that grave old adage: If you didn't chart it, you didn't do it. You see, there is plenty I do in any given encounter with a patient that never makes it into words, much less onto paper. This is not petty stuff either; it is at the heart of my work, for effective nursing, even in this age of technology, depends upon the skilled recognition, interpretation, and use of nonverbal phenomena and apparent irrelevancies.

When Kimi Morgan came in with her two-month-old, for exam-ple, there was a lot more to our encounter than would meet your eye in the chart. What you see is a SOAP note for an uncomplicated upper respiratory infection. That is all I am held accountable for by my peers, the third-party payer, the courts — and Kimi herself, for that matter. But the fact is that the URI was not what I spent most of my time on. Just watching Kimi with Danny as we chatted about the outfit she was wearing (her wardrobe and personal style had been the envy of all her friends at high school last year), I realized how uncomfortable she still was with her maternity. She held the baby stiffly, at arm's length, never making eye contact. When he began to cry, she spoke to him sharply as she searched her tote bag frantically for a bottle. I said nothing while she rummaged, but took Danny, held him close and face to face, then made as if to toss him up into the air. Startled, the baby stopped crying and gazed at me, so we baby-talked for a while. When Kimi (who had been watching all this) was ready with the bottle, I put him back into her arms, tucking his blanket around him with much ado. "What a baby!" I said with enthusiasm, patting her on the back. "What does his daddy have to say?" With that, the conversation picked up again.

I did not express my concern about Kimi's parenting either during our consultation or afterwards in the chart (I was using a URI form, after all). Nor did I pass on any child care tips. I did stroke the baby again before they left and encouraged her to schedule a well child visit as soon as he was better. I told her once more how great she looked and mentioned that now might be a time to make that appointment to talk family planning. Only after Kimi had gone did I articulate my belief that this baby's health was threatened, and not by a virus. Sharon and I agreed to follow up fast in the event Kimi should fail to show up in two weeks "for Danny's shots."

Putting illness in context of a complex of lives, touching the untouched, cutting through words with silence — these are only a few of the ways nurses nurse. But they do not find full expression in formal professional discourse simply because they take place in a wordless medium. Like music. A piece of music can be described in words but reading

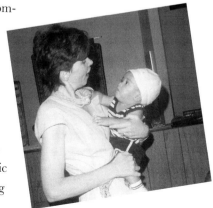

the description is in no way like hearing the music. The same is true of nursing.

So how do I reconcile the art of nursing with its practice in a world preoccupied with science and technology? To the extent that it is possible, I have to coax the nonverbal into words. It requires commitment, talent, and hard work. But it is perhaps the only way to attract an audience and build a constituency for nursing. So what if it takes an extra piece of paper and more of my time to document my encounter with Kimi and Danny fully. So get it and start writing!

Then, of course, there's that irrational, nonverbal attempt at communication I use if only to satisfy myself. Pull Kimi and Danny's charts from the file and look at them. I don't say read them, because the words inside cannot tell you all I want you to know. I say look at them. They're neat, clean, functional, whole. They represent in some crude way what I want for Kimi and Danny. Looking at their charts, can you see how well I've nursed them?

Inner-city Washington has many mom-and-pop convenience stores. Although I don't know any other mom-and-pop clinics, I'm thinking that we deserve some study because, like the convenience stores, we serve an important function.

The thought about mom-and-pops came to me as I sat in Room 2 at the clinic listening to Ruth Jefferson talk about the many stressors that she thought were driving her blood pressure up and her weight down. First there were her grown children, all but one of whom had lost their way in life, leaving her with seven grandchildren to raise. Then there was the mom-and-pop store she and her husband had owned and run for the past twenty years. "I'm there day and night in all kinds of weather," she said. "I wasn't even sure I should close up long enough to come over and get my pressure checked because I might lose a customer — but still, we barely make ends meet."

"How do you manage at all?" I asked, not wanting to shift the focus from her but unable to contain my curiosity about the mom-and-pop stores scattered around this part of town. Some, like hers, survive literally in the shadow of a sleek new Giant supermarket, the neighborhood showplace. "Well," Ms. Jefferson said, adjusting her glasses with a quick, nervous gesture, "We're convenient, especially if you only need a few items. No long lines. And we just stock the main things — Pampers and Tide, Wonder Bread and Hostess cakes, beer and sodas, candy, canned goods, those microwave sandwiches…It's more personal, too. Parents can send their children and know I'll send them home with the right order and the right change. And," here she smiled ruefully, "we still give credit."

That conversation with Ruth Jefferson and my subsequent visits to Columbia Grocery to buy cold sodas and chat with whichever family members were tending the store was how I came to see Community Medical Care, the clinic where I work, as a mom-and-pop store within the health care system. We're small, located in a residential area, and offer a familiar array of "the main things." You can come for one or two, although you may leave with more. We're personal—we'll remember you if you come a couple of times—and you'll get to know the five of us, including our children, who are often around. Of course we give credit, discounts too. Like Columbia Grocery, which faces competition from supermarkets, smaller chain stores on the order of 7-Elevens, and gourmet shops that serve the growing number of middle class "urban pioneers," CMC lives in the shadow of our "competitors": hospitals, government and hospital-run clinics, and the glittery, expensive specialty practices that neighborhood residents with insurance and bus fare may decide to patronize in order to get "the best." Like Columbia Grocery, we worry about money and our chances of survival, even after twelve years on Ninth Street.

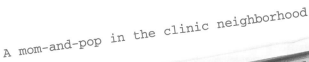

A mom-and-pop in the clinic neighborhood

But the most striking part of the comparison is that we actually have mom-and-pop in the roles of nurse and doctor. Pop likes to cogitate, read up on new products and talk them over with the salesmen that have him on their route or other small businessmen he knows. He'll fix on a problem until he's solved it, whether a piece of equipment on the blink, a system that could be improved, or a customer's request. He deals in "what-ifs" and "therefores." Sometimes he gets lost in his thoughts and forgets for a moment about a customer still waiting. That's probably why Mom works out front more often (luckily, we have more than one "Mom").

Mom can solve problems, too, but her greatest contribution is engaging the customer, finding out what the customer really wants, explaining the various products, even telling the customer about things she may not stock but that can be made at home or found elsewhere. She looks out for the customer's pocketbook. She doesn't forget to ask about the new baby, the job, or a favorite TV show. She always says goodbye with a heartfelt, "You come back and see us when you need something." And people do, because they feel good about the place.

This city has many mom-and-pop groceries, most of them in poor neighborhoods, but I don't know any other mom-and-pop clinics. Are we an anachronism? Or simply a rare species not well enough understood to make the "endangered" lists? I'm thinking that we deserve some study for, like all mom-and-pops, we serve an important function especially for the poor. Many of our "customers" are intimidated by big supermarkets. Some can't read. That makes it hard to find your way around, weigh the claims of competing brands, or understand innova-tions like unit pricing. They prefer a place where you don't get lost in the aisles, can ask for what you want, recognize the brand you're sold, and feel free to return it if there's something wrong with it. There are other practical considerations. When you're poor, you can't afford to buy in advance of need or even to shop for a week at a time. You need credit to tide you over until money comes in. When you have a houseful of children or are handicapped, you need to be able to send out a child unaccompanied or get someone to deliver to the house. Mom-and-pops accommodate. They know you. They understand your situation because, more often than not, they share it. Our mom-and-pop clinic works the same way.

What would happen if more of those who patronize mom-and-pop groceries also had access to mom-and-pop clinics like ours? Efforts to incorporate them into large, impersonal, and complicated systems like medical centers, HMOs, and traditional government clinics have not, on the whole, been successful. Is it because they get lost in the aisles? Can't find "the main things?" Don't have the cash?

I concede that finding enough moms-and-pops willing and able to risk starting a "family" business would be the first problem. Having solved that, the next challenge would be establishing their place in the health care system. Believe me, in this day and age, if you don't have a link to a hospital and don't fit into a recognizable category (like a 7-Eleven, say), you face formidable obstacles in responding to your patients' more complex needs. Anyhow, it's a thought. The kind you have while strolling over to Columbia Grocery for a cold soda.

Here is an excerpt from a fund-raising letter I
wrote in 1990. I include it because it describes the
move from Ninth & P back to our original "home" on
Ninth & L and provides context for some of the essays
that follow.

Remember this sketch?* Jim Hall made it for the cover of Community
Medical Care's last annual report which you received before Christmas.

In it, we wrote about the slow but sure process of gentrification
in the clinic neighborhood and some of our patients, displaced by renovation, who are searching for a way home.

Never, in deciding on the title for the report, did we imagine that
we, too, would be finding a way home. But we are.

Trace a finger down Ninth Street from P, where we are now, to L
and you'll be at "the old clinic" the place we leased in April 1978 and left
in January 1982 when our landlord made us a buy or move offer. We
couldn't afford to buy so we moved, just like our patients have to do.
But our story will have an unexpected and happy ending.

A series of events too long to tell here led us back to our original
landlord who has invited us to lease 1118 Ninth Street once again. "You
were wonderful tenants," she tells us. "And remember, that place was
made for you!"

Indeed it was. Jim Hall designed it and it hasn't changed substantially in the eight years we've been away. It will be better managed than our
present space and, we reckon, a bit cheaper. It will be more accessible to
our handicapped patients. And we will have a much needed fourth
examination room.

We all agree that we should seize this opportunity to move. We have the energy. All we need is the money — for the security deposit, floor and window coverings, dry wall in at least one area, equipment and furnishings for the new exam room and all the unavoidable expense that goes with any move.

This will cost about $6000. The New Community Church has made a significant contribution: $3000. Can you help us with the rest?

We don't like to come to you more than once a year with our annual report and discrete (we hope) request for money. But this is an exceptional year for us — and we believe you should have the opportunity to make an exceptional contribution!

Moving in June is our goal. Already the word is out, especially among the patients who knew us back when. "Well, that's a blessing," one elderly, arthritic lady said. It's a blessing for her because the only way she could make it up the steep steps outside our present office was with a substantial boost from behind.

We feel blessed, too — to be finding a way home.

* The sketch, which I've always thought portrayed us so well, is on the front cover of this book. Jim recalls making the first draft on a napkin in a French restaurant on 18th Street.

If I had to pick a tool that represents me as a nurse, it would not be a stethoscope, syringe, or computer monitor. I might choose reading glasses, a telephone, a coffee cup...

I was roaming the aisles of one of those huge, free-standing toy outlets you find on the outskirts of cities in search of a birthday present for a school-age child, when my eye lit on something familiar, high up on a steep bank of shelves. It was a play doctor kit. No, wait. There was a doctor kit and a nurse kit. My curiosity piqued, I pushed a rolling stepladder down the aisle and climbed up to examine my find.

First, the doctor kit. As I opened it, I remembered the time in my own childhood when some friends and I pooled all the money we had earned selling homemade potholders to buy a bottle of iodine from the drugstore. We spent the afternoon dressing imaginary wounds. What a shame! No iodine inside the doctor kit. What it did contain was a canvas bag, stethoscope, reflex hammer, thermometer, syringe, scalpel, small plastic basin, band-aid, box of cotton, eye chart, eye glasses, a red cross sign, an office sign, an identification card, and name badge. Fair enough, I thought. Now what could be in the nurse kit?

I replaced the box with the picture of the boy-doctor on the outside and picked up the one with the girl-nurse. I opened it and found that except for the RN on the identification card and name badge, the contents of the nurse kit were identical!

I've thought a lot about these toys since my shopping expedition. At first I was mainly concerned with what they teach children—that nursing and doctoring are the same except that if you're a girl you're the nurse and, if a boy, the doctor. Then I began to think about the adults who designed the kits. Is this what they believe, too? Did they check with members of both professions before deciding what to include? Or did they just want to avoid fights between future nurses and doctors: "Hey, how come you got a knife and I only got this plastic bowl?"

Well then, I asked myself, what would you put in a doctor kit and, more to the point, a nurse kit? As I sorted through the possibilities I realized I was worried that my nurse kit wouldn't be as interesting or relevant to a child's interests as the doctor kit. The lighthearted suggestions of some of the nurses I polled confirmed my fears ("lotion," "an ice pack," "a washcloth").

One day I had a flash of inspiration. Both Jim, my physician colleague at the clinic, and I have "medical" bags we carry when we make home visits. Why not compare what's in his bag with what's in mine? Maybe that will tell something about the tools of our trades. This is what I discovered: The core contents of each of our bags are, in fact, similar. We both carry a stethoscope, blood pressure cuff, thermometer, syringes, blood collection apparatus, a reflex hammer and other neurological testing equipment, and an assortment of dressing supplies (I carry a larger selection than he does). In addition, Jim's bag has scalpels, glass slides, cytology fixative, culture tubes, multi-puncture TB tests, and an array of pills: digoxin, Dilantin, antibiotics, and antihistamines. In contrast, my bag has rubber gloves and lubricant, bandage scissors, nail clippers, a flashlight, tape measure, and apron. It doesn't stop there. The trunk of my car, where the bag resides when not in use, has turned into a branch office of sorts. In it, you'll find a bathroom scale, plastic bags, paper towels, elastic bandages, Unna boots for stasis ulcers and, depending on whom I happen to be nursing, anything from an alternating pressure mattress and electrocardiograph machine to sheets, towels, groceries, and bottled water.

As for the tools Jim and I use in the office, they are largely the same. It is possible that Jim uses more laboratory equipment and I use more health education materials, but I cannot be certain. I remember the photo layout of a brochure we produced several years ago when we were marketing our services. There were shots of each of us with a syringe. He was doing a fine needle aspiration biopsy on an adult and I was giving an immunization to a child. Then we had a picture of Jim examining a slide under the microscope and one of me examining a patient's ulcerated foot. In the last photograph, the two of us were sitting around a table in conversation with a patient. We felt the photographs presented a balanced picture of who we were and what we did.

Upon reflection, I would have to say that, in the areas of practice where we use different tools, Jim's are associated with technology as symbolized by the white lab coat he wears in the office. Mine are more closely associated with domesticity, like the bib apron I wear when I wear any cover-up at all. Yet even when my tools are the things of everyday, they have specialized purposes and my use of them is informed by my knowledge of science and the healing art. I may use a scale to monitor fluid retention, a basin to treat a skin ulcer, supplemental food to enhance the body's ability to heal, and gloves and lubricant to—how shall I put it— clear the distal end of the intestinal tract.

If I had to pick a tool that represents me as a nurse, you can be sure it would not be a stethoscope or computer screen. I might choose the reading glasses that I put on to consult my reference books or examine a part of the body and take off when I am preparing to listen to a patient. I might choose a telephone to convey accessibility or even a coffee cup to project warmth and hospitality. Once when two colleagues and I were talking about opening a drop-in nursing center, we decided we wanted to create the atmosphere of a friendly kitchen where patients would feel more like neighbors who had stopped by with a question or concern.

But how do you convey the stuff of nursing to a child? I say a kit is not the answer. Leave that to the junior doctors. Nursing has more to do with people than with things. So how about picture books, puppets, stories, videos—any medium that can give life to characters and situations, words, and actions. And what child can resist it, that tantalizing phrase, "Once upon a time there was a nurse…"

When I'm sick, I would like to know she is there, not necessarily at my bedside, but on the spot if there is trouble. Big Nurse could say it any way she wanted to, but her message would be blunt and true: "Look, I'm in charge. Everything's going to be all right."

I am sitting with a group of doctors and nurses who are talking earnestly about a subject that concerns them all: doctors and nurses. One doctor, who looks to be about sixty, has the floor. "What I really miss when I come onto a ward," he says with feeling, "is the good, old-fashioned head nurse. Someone I know. Someone I can consider a peer. Someone — I'll come right out and say it — someone closer to my own age. As it is, I have to run a whole gamut of nursing personnel and none of them may know exactly what's going on with my patient."

After the first flush of defensiveness subsides, I have to admit to myself I know what he is talking about. I am one who believed that the movement toward decentralization of nursing authority was a good idea, but I make hospital visits, too, when our clinic patients are hospitalized and I have the same problem my physician colleague does. I've always assumed the reason I feel so frustrated trying to establish contact with the nurse responsible for my patients' care — or even to get basic information about their condition — is that I am an outsider, don't know how the units are organized, and am generally reluctant to demand an audience with "whoever is in charge here."

Even hospital nurses must know how it feels to approach the nurses' station of a hospital that is not their own. There are people everywhere, none of them charged with attending to you. They are uniformed in any number of ways — scrubs, a lab coat over streetwear, a "civilian" top and uniform-style bottoms or vice versa, once in a while a person in white. They all seem young. Who are the nurses? Is there a ward clerk or unit manager? Is the only person whose eye you are able to catch really the chaplain or a messenger from Admitting? If there are name badges, you can't read them, nor do they tell you much about the wearer. The person who finally responds to your questions about your patient may or may not know anything about him or her firsthand. I can't remember when I last had the privilege of speaking with either a primary nurse, team leader, or nurse in charge — and knew it at the time.

Recently I had an opportunity to get a patient's-eye view of one nursing unit in a large teaching hospital in the Washington area. All my nursing savvy and detective work were of no help in trying to decipher the workings of the place from my hospital bed. Persons in uniform came and went. Only two ever introduced themselves as my nurse, but I still didn't know whether it was for an eight, ten, or twelve-hour shift, or for my entire stay. I don't remember seeing the same staff two days in a row. Once I was able to pick out a person in charge because she came to see my roommate about a complaint my roommate had made. Identifying this person in charge (of the unit? of the service? of the hospital?) posed a real challenge since she was wearing a costume, not a uniform. Somewhat disoriented, I had forgotten that it was Halloween and congratulated myself when I was able at last to make sense out of what seemed a bizarre turn of events: a high-power, high-tech nursing unit run by an elf.

On the whole, I had an uneventful stay. Someone — many someones — were undoubtedly looking out for me. But there was one night, one miserable hour or two, when the pain control device I clung to with full, albeit misplaced confidence failed. It was a glitch — glitches happen. The nurse who responded to my visitor's summons — I was able to make out "Marie" and "RN" on her name badge — took in the facts of the situation and, in the end, did the right thing. She called

someone to fix it. Meantime I was lapsing into a state I hate to have
to describe as hysteria, but may as well. Marie was concerned, I knew
that from the expression on her face. She was also anxious, returning
every few minutes to ask if, by chance, I was any more comfortable.
What I most wanted during that interminable interval I was able to
articulate only later. It wasn't just compassion. It wasn't the cool hand
on the fevered brow. What I wanted was Big Nurse. Big Nurse could
say it any way she wanted to, but the message would be blunt and true:
"Look, I'm in charge. Calm down and leave it to me. Everything's
going to be all right."

When I got home from the hospital, I checked out Ken Kesey's
book from the library and reread it. Big Nurse, as he describes her
in *One Flew Over the Cuckoo's Nest* [18], is pathologically obsessed with
the control of her ward — staff as well as patients — in a large mental
hospital. Her use of authority is destructive. So compelling was her
portrayal in the book that Big Nurse has entered the language as a
colloquialism for the dominating woman.

But let's examine Big Nurse for a minute. If nothing else, she has
presence. "Her uniform, even after she's been here half a day, is still
starched so stiff it don't exactly bend any place," the narrator says.
"It cracks sharp at the joints with a sound like a frozen canvas being
folded." Forget the starch, but remember, there is no one in the institu-
tion who doesn't recognize Big Nurse and know that she is in charge.

"Her face is...calm, as though she had a cast made and painted
to just the look she wants. Confident, patient, and unruffled." I
wouldn't have minded seeing such a face from my hospital bed. And
I wouldn't have minded knowing this about her: "The Big Nurse gets
real put out if anything keeps her outfit from running smooth...."

I don't know what my doctor friend would say but I, for one,
think that professional nursing should take a serious look at Big Nurse.
She needs rehabilitation, sure. She also needs updating. What I have

in mind is the picture of a mature nurse, immediately recognizable as an authority figure, at the scene of the action, and concerned above all with the welfare of those in her charge. Is this the good, old-fashioned head nurse? I don't know. I do know that I would like her to stand out in the maze of the modern hospital. And, when I'm sick, I would like to know she is there, not necessarily at my bedside, but on the spot if there is trouble. To anyone who cares to listen I say, bring back Big Nurse.

Big Nurse as drawn by one of the clinic children

Even as an anxious patient, I was aware of the tyranny
of the time slot in a busy medical practice. "How much
time do I have?" I asked the specialist. I vowed I
would never forget the medicinal power of his response.

My colleague Natalie is working per diem on a GYN oncology ward while
she decides what to do with her professional life. She has gotten to know the
regular nurses and the pressures they work under—short staffing seems to
be at the root of most of them. In a brief conversation over a stand-up
lunch, one of the staff nurses opened up to Natalie. "You can imagine the
emotional needs these women have," the nurse said. "They're bubbling to
the surface all the time, just begging to be addressed. We know they're
there—it haunts us. But you know what? We don't have enough time even
to give the kind of physical care we want to. We can't begin to deal with the
rest. I'll be honest with you. We've gotten so we just don't ask the question."

Asking the question. I know what it means: opening a safe but wide
open space into which patients can let their burdens tumble. It means offering to hear the last word in a person's heart. Asking the question is easy.
You can say something as simple as "How are you today?" and, if you look
like you really want to know, your patient feels the space opening up
around her, drawing out what is inside like a delicate siphon. It's responding
that requires time, attention, and skill.

In my work at Community Medical Care, it sometimes happens that
I've asked The Question without realizing it. My challenge, one I admit I
am not always able to meet, is to set aside my own agenda and timetable
for the encounter and make room for whatever is about to happen.
The other day, Katrina Barry came in for her routine blood pressure
check. Fifteen or twenty minutes, maximum, is how long this should take.
I came into the exam room, sat down, greeted her, glanced at the chart,

noticed that her blood pressure was up, then, quite inadvertently, asked The Question. "Did you start the new pills?" I asked. "No," she said in a quavery voice. "I have to tell you the truth, I didn't. I didn't even get the prescription filled because there was no money to do it. I lost my job. See, I quit because I had a better offer somewhere else, but when I showed up to start the new job, they decided not to hire me. And, of course, my old job wouldn't take me back because of my not giving two weeks notice. I'm way behind on my rent and now my daughter's got pregnant and moved in with me—there's hardly enough room for one. I was hoping to get a better place, but what little savings I had has to go to feeding us and paying her doctor bills. I'm so depressed I can hardly get out of bed. I didn't think I could make it here today, but with this awful headache, I had to do something…"

Forty minutes later, as we were coming out of the exam room, Ms. Barry said, "Thanks for the shoulder." It had taken all the courage I had to listen, knowing that hearing her was all I could do. And even then, I had to keep pulling my mind back from the waiting room where my next patient was probably starting to ask what time it was, from my desk where charts and telephone messages were stacking up, and my kitchen at home where no one had made any plans for dinner.

Ms. Barry is not one of those people who can deliver an oration in answer to a yes-or-no question like "Any allergies?" She is not one you would hesitate to ask if there was anything else on her mind. She is definitely not in the league with Mr. Mims whose yearly physical took three separate appointments because I couldn't get a word, or a tongue blade, in edgewise. The encounter with Katrina Barry called to mind a personal experience that, I hope, has left its mark on my own practice.

I was seeking a second opinion on a serious medical problem. The specialist seated across the desk from me was someone I did not know. I had stuck a manila folder full of lab and X-ray reports under one arm while I thumbed the pages of a yellow legal pad for the list of questions and issues I wanted to cover. I was very nervous and very scared. "How much time do I have?" I asked, looking at my watch. At Community Medical Care, the appointment book often looms like a disinterested tyrant over our activities, granting so much time for this, so much for that. I knew it was the same in most offices. I needed to know, needed to fit my hopes and fears and thirst for answers into whatever time slot his appointment book had allotted to me.

"How much time do I have?" I asked, mentally prepared to move fast. I had no more than uncapped my pen when I heard him say gently, "All the time you need." Then he sat back and waited. I was stunned. I'd had no such expectations. My "very nervous" and "very scared" came out in a rush like air from a deflating blood pressure cuff. I don't know what that response cost him in terms of time, but for me, the healing had begun. I vowed I would never forget the medicinal power of the words "all the time you need."

I wouldn't know what to say to the nurses on Natalie's ward. I do know that nursing is as dependent upon time as medicine is upon technology. True, both need both, but for nursing, time is of the essence. The patients in that high-stress environment might have been doctored, but it doesn't sound as if they've been nursed.

I suppose my challenges are of a lesser order. If I run late, other patients may be delayed and teammates may have to work overtime. Still, I have that option. The other day we squeezed in an appointment for a longtime patient. "It's a quickie," said Sharon, who had taken the call. At five minutes to five I called Arlene back to the exam room. Even before she sat down I could see that her eyes were puffy and she was brushing away tears. "Well?" I said, asking The Question. "I know it's almost five," she said. "Do you want the long version or the short version?" She tried to smile. I made a point of taking off my glasses and getting into a comfortable position. "Why don't you just start in," I said as gently as I could, thinking back to another time and place. "Take all the time you need."

I had nursed stroke patients. Their care held no
mysteries for me—until I read William Stafford's poem.
I became convinced that only if I understood what that
poem was saying, could I really nurse a stroke patient.

It was the Sixties and I was a student of everything. I had an associate
degree in nursing and a year of hospital experience under my belt.
I had moved to the California Bay Area and enrolled first at University
of California, Berkeley, then at the Medical Center campus in San
Francisco. I was drenched in new knowledge. I felt shiny and new and
very wise. I was twenty-one.

There was a paperback book of poetry I used to carry around with
me. In it, I found a short poem by William Stafford called "Strokes."[19]
It began like this:

The left side of her world is gone—
the rest sustained by memory
and a realization: There are still the children.

Now I had nursed stroke patients. Their care held no mysteries for
me—until I read the poem. The more I read it, the more I became
convinced that only if I really, truly understood what that poem was
saying, could I nurse a stroke patient—really, truly. This certainty grew
inside me until I could scarcely contain it.

That semester I was taking Psych 110 with Louis Schaw, an *enfant
terrible* who used to play the class with the same diabolical skill that
Paganini is said to have played the violin. In discussion, he would lure
you down a path you'd never taken before, through dense thickets,
across vast plains, up high mountains, then, without warning, just as you
were about to reach the summit, he'd turn on you and challenge your
right to be there. I seldom spoke in class. But one afternoon, when the

topic had turned to what nursing is, my hand shot up, my mouth opened, and I heard myself telling about the poem and what it had taught me about nursing.

Dr. Schaw allowed the briefest of silences after I had finished, then fixed me in his sights. "Aren't you being rather naive?" he asked. And he went on to describe the command of technology and the skills one needs to make the diagnosis of CVA, stabilize the patient's vital signs, restore function, and prevent complications and further physical loss. An admirable display of medical expertise for a professor of psychology!

I was struck dumb. What he said was true. But was it the whole truth? Instead of letting go, I only held on tighter to my revelation. I knew what I knew. But it would be my secret. In the years that followed, I did not run across any other poems or works of art that had the same impact on me. I remember reading Kafka's "Metamorphosis" in a graduate nursing course at the University of Washington, but I had trouble relating it to the care of patients who, in my experience, rarely turned into cockroaches. After graduate school, I drifted away from hands-on nursing. I would see occasional references in the literature to a novel or short story of use in helping students acquire empathy with patients. None of these works were actually written by nurses. I didn't find that remarkable. Then.

By 1980, I was back again, a clinician involved in hospice care, home care, and primary health care. I found myself brooding about patients who troubled or perplexed me. There was one in particular, an elderly woman, poor, bed-bound, living alone in a rundown house that strangers used to deal and shoot drugs. More than one health professional counseled me to withdraw my services and "precipitate a crisis" so that the city could step in and force her into a nursing home "where she belonged." And yet, there was something about this woman that was compelling: she had expectations. She owned her own home and owned her grave plot and planned to go from one to the other

when the Lord called her. Not before. One evening after dinner,
utterly frustrated, I pulled out my journal and began to write:

> *Just*
> *who do you think you are, Maggie Jones*
> *following me home from work*
> *insinuating yourself into my evening*
> *shading my thoughts?*

Over time, Maggie turned into a long, narrative poem. And as
she did, I began to understand her, and myself when I was with her.
I believe that as a result, I was able to nurse her really, truly.

After Maggie, other patients of mine, past and present, started
turning into poems. It could happen at any time, without warning, like
the day Aretha Robbins, in the depths of depression, and I sat talking
at her kitchen table:

> *There are three ways to do it*
> *she says at last*
> > *Do what? I ask*
> *jump out the window,*
> *poison or…you know…*
> > *What do I know?*
> *This! she says*
> *and flicks one scarred wrist*
> *with a whisk*
> *of the other hand.*

It's art — my own poetry for the most part — that enables me to nurse
Carol with AIDS, Maria with chronic pelvic pain, and Curtis
who, at eight, has never tasted grapes, or love. It's art that sustains me
in a profession that many of my colleagues contemplate leaving.
It's art that expresses what drew me to nursing in the first place and

connects me with every other nurse. I submit that the heart of nursing is the art of nursing and, to quote Wordsworth, "we have given our hearts away." We've sold out to technology, like everyone else.

We are two million strong—and that doesn't count practical nurses and nursing assistants, who also nurse. We work in every nook and cranny of the health care system. We have researchers, educators, managers, clinical specialists. We have politicians, pundits, and entrepreneurs. What we need now are a few poets, playwrights, visual artists, and maybe a musician or two. To nurse—really, truly—is art, and our art holds the power we need to unite us, keep us going, move us forward. It's time, high time, to unleash it.

Maggie

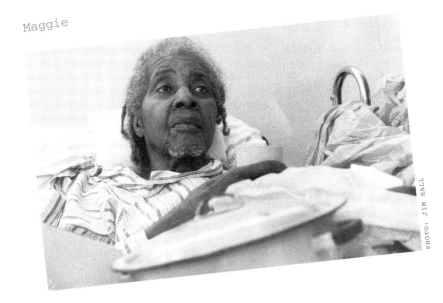

PHOTO: JIM HALL

Maggie was one of those patients whose life changed
mine. In this poem, she speaks for herself.

Just
who do you think you are, Maggie Jones
following me home from work
insinuating yourself into my evening
shading my thoughts?

Just
who do you think you are
lying flat as a pancake in the middle of your bed
your world ranged around you in brown paper bags?

(Rather like a dead Pharaoh in his tomb, I'd say
buried with all his treasure)

So you fell one day and had to be taken
    to the hospital.
You didn't break any bones, after all.
You came home in a taxi
climbed the steep flight of stairs to your room
took to your bed and stayed there.
That was three years ago, Maggie
three years with only one thing to look forward to—
    livin'.

I'm here by the hand of the Lord, you always say
    when I come
    though the hand of the Lord didn't smite the rat
    that bit your foot
    that cold winter day last year
    as it foraged in your sheets for bread and jelly.
I guess it'll be all right
    you said in your genteel way
    looking up at me with soft doe eyes as I dressed
    the wound that brought us together.

Why don't you go to a home? we ask, shocked
    to see the condition you're in
    (the church ladies, the social worker
    your niece, your nephew, and I).
Because I still have my right mind
    you say simply.

    A nursing home is no place
    for someone who still has their mind.

But it's not safe here, we say
    (the church ladies, the social worker
    your niece, your nephew, and I).
Don't you know they shoot drugs
    and people in this neighborhood?
I've never been bothered
    you say, matter-of-factly.

What about fire? we say
    (the church ladies, the social worker
    your niece, your nephew, and I).
There was a fire once, and the fireman carried me out.
I own my home and I own my grave plot
    and I plan to go from one to the other
    when the Lord calls me
    you say quietly, clutching a packet
    of long, white envelopes.

But now your gas is cut off
    until you come up with $700.
You're lucky it's not freezing and there's an electric
    coffee maker we can use to heat water to wash you.
I guess the money will come from somewhere
    you say, looking at me steadily.

And Meals on Wheels has cut you off because it's a bad
    neighborhood to begin with and then
    the front door fell off its hinges
    onto the Meals on Wheels delivery lady.
I guess there's enough food in the United States
    to feed me
    you say, looking at me knowingly.

And they've taken away your homemaker because they say
    you need more care
    than the agency can give.
I guess things will work out
    you say, looking at me trustingly.

How can you lie there and say, serenely, you guess
    things will work out?

Your room is cold
    your sheets are soaked with urine
    your skin is bleeding from bedsores
    you don't know where your next meal is coming from
    you're a poor old lady
        hidden away
        in a falling-down house
        in a no-good neighborhood.
    And you have expectations?

You told your niece not to worry about you
    the nurse was coming.
Hey, Maggie Jones, don't wait for me, don't count on me.
    I'll bathe you
    dress your wounds
    treat your minor ailments
    even do your laundry and bring you food
    once in a while.
But save you?
God alone —the hand of the Lord—can save you.

I see you now in my mind's eye and wonder
    as I sit
    after dinner
    in my warm house
    on a safe street
    in a good neighborhood
Just
    who do you think you are, Maggie Jones?

In that pivotal moment of her life, I was not pro-life or pro-choice. I was pro-Lisa. I wanted to be her midwife in the original sense of the word—"with woman."

Nadine and I are members of the same church in inner-city Washington. She'd been wanting to visit Community Medical Care, and I wanted to hear more about the pregnancy crisis center she manages. We both serve the same low-income population and figured our organizations ought to be referring back and forth. It was a bright spring day when she finally made it over to the clinic, the day after the Supreme Court ruled to uphold a ban on abortion counseling at federally subsidized family planning clinics. I had been thinking about it all morning.

I didn't know whether her organization received federal money or not. "So how does the Supreme Court decision affect you?" I asked after we had settled down to talk. "Oh, not at all," she said. "The organization that runs the center is very conservative. We don't deal with abortion. It's awfully hard not to, though. I've found that more and more. That's one of the reasons I'm glad I'm doing administration now and not actual counseling."

"What about you?" she asked. "Are you pro-life or pro-choice?" I wasn't sure whether she was asking about CMC or me personally. In neither case could I give a simple answer. I remember staff discussions in the early days of the clinic. We really struggled with the subject of abortion and what we would tell pregnant women who asked about it. We were not in agreement then and probably would not be now. In theory, that is. What none of us had reckoned with in the beginning was the sheer power of Real Life to strip one of illusions, euphemisms, even ideals. There are no taboos in the clinic. This is not our policy. It's simply a fact. Countless conversations start off with, "I'm not gonna lie to you," and move off relentlessly into stories of drugs, sex, suicide, child abuse, murder — and every other form of violence. We don't have the luxury of keeping our focus narrow and our hearts pure.

The drama that surrounds pregnancy testing is a perfect example. In the clinic neighborhood, as in most of the rest of the world, a woman's fertility is the basis of her self-esteem, and pregnancy, the centerpiece of her life. The women we see have no distractions like money, career, or even marriage to occupy them, and few opportunities for travel or other kinds of invigorating change. A girl turning fourteen or fifteen is less likely to be asked questions like "What are you going to get?" by her friends than something like, "You gonna let him break you for your birthday?"

Among the women we see, pregnancy, like everything else in life, is not something you plan, it's something that happens to you. You may want it fervently or fear it desperately, but you don't control it. You react. That's why contraception doesn't seem to work for the majority of the women who come to CMC. They flirt with it for a while, take a pack or two of pills, but usually admit failure with what seem the flimsiest of excuses. "I just don't feel right when I take those things," is a common one. It's a polite way of saying, "No thanks. I'll take my chances."

I am thinking back to some pregnancy tests I did last week. Before each of them, I remembered to ask my patient, "If this comes out positive, will it be good news, bad news, or just — news?" That's how I know what expression to wear when I tell her the results. Margarita was first. Thirty-five years old with four children in Salvador, she had met a new man in this country. He wanted her to bear his child and she wanted to cement the relationship. Bingo! A blue dot means the test is positive. *"¡Gracias, Doctora!"* she says with a radiant smile. *"¡Gracias!"*

Norma's was next. I have known her for years, including the one when she had the abortion that devastated her. That bitter memory forms part of the bond between us. Now her period was late. "Please, God," she breathes, "I'll never miss a pill again, I swear. Please let it be negative." It is. "Thank you Jesus, thank you!"

Laverne has had twelve pregnancies, eight kids. She tried to get her tubes tied right after the last one, but in the hospital they told her no, she would have to come back and have it done later. Now how was she going to arrange that, she asked no one in particular? This test was positive. Well, Medicaid doesn't pay for abortions anymore, so that's that. What's one more in an extended family household with eighteen children and who knows how many adults? Yeah, she's back on drugs. ("I'm not gonna lie to you.") She needs to go now, the baby's crying and she's forgotten his bottle.

Toni is eighteen and her friends are teasing her because she's never been pregnant. Her period's not late, but she's sleeping a lot and gaining weight—everyone tells her so. Could she be pregnant? No, not this time. Nor is Sondra, a regular customer who comes with her new man. "He's a trip," she confides. "Every little thing that happens—I get a stomachache, maybe—and he's just sure I'm pregnant. Makes me come down here to get checked out."

Then there was Lisa. Positive. "I'm tellin' you how I feel," she said, looking away. "I'm not gonna have this baby. I just got a new job and my friend's in jail. I'm going through too many changes. No way can I have it. Is it true that an abortion can mess you up later? That's what someone told me. How do they do it? Does it hurt bad? I'm really scared."

I did not say to Lisa in that most important and perhaps pivotal moment of her life, "We do not consider abortion an appropriate method of family planning." She hadn't claimed it was. I answered her questions, listened as hard as I could, and helped her make a plan. Because in that moment, I was not pro-life or pro-choice. I was pro-Lisa. I wanted to be her midwife in the original sense of the word—"with woman."

This is what I tried to explain to Nadine as we sat in my office at the clinic, talking about Real Life and the Supreme Court. She nodded.

"I guess you're glad you don't get federal money then," she said. "You're right about that," I answered.

Our Children

Teresa's poem contrasts her own family life with that
of so many families in the CMC neighborhood who live in
"a world that seems violent, troubled and confused."

For three days she labored
alone in the delivery room.
Her husband paced the hallway.
In those days there were no coaches,
no rooming in, no birth plans.
And then, the waiting was over.
A baby girl was born.
Years later, my mother will tell me
"We were so happy the day you were born.
Oh, how we wanted a girl!"

    "I don't know if I can
    keep this baby."
    Carla, a mother of three young boys
    is talking with Sharon.
    Carla is the voice and legs
    for a large extended family.
    In one week's time, her infant son
    was hospitalized, her mother
    was diagnosed with cancer, and
    she learned she was pregnant.
    "I don't know what to do,"
    she cries, "I don't know
    what to do."

"Chocolate milk and a book, Daddy!"
Megan, my niece rests in her bed
clutching her silkie—a worn
peach blanket with satin trim.
"The cat sleeps on my chest
and put Strawberry next to my pillow.
If I imagine happy thoughts,
I won't have bad dreams."

A child's cry pierces the night.
Shayla wakes up in a cold sweat.
Three years old.
I wonder about night terrors.
"When did it start?"
I ask her mother.
"Started when the gangs moved in.
At night the shootings are so bad
we crouch to the floor and
crawl to the bathroom.
The children sleep in the tub—
It's the safest place in the house.

In the past year
the violence has edged
closer to the lives of our families.
Kayla, a three-year-old, fell
to her death from an open window.
Daryl, an eighteen-month-old, was thrown
from the balcony
of a fourth floor apartment.
Paco was gunned down
in a barber's chair
and the list goes on.

Somehow we know
that life is not fair
and yet we want to believe
that it can and should be.
For years I have struggled
with the contrast between
a world of safety, family, and love
and a world that seems
violent, troubled, and confused.
My heart aches for the children
caught in the web of poverty.
    So many unanswered questions.

For now I hold onto
that which I know to be true.
Healing takes place
moment by moment
over long periods of time.
The presence of a caring soul
    to listen
    to touch
    to comfort
    to offer a tissue
    to hug
    to trust
    to ask how you are
        over and over again
in time
brings new life.

Any nurse knows how we work almost anonymously, enveloped within the folds of a hospital or community agency. But I'm still astonished to hear my patients, when asked where they go for health care, say, "Dr. Hall." Some have never seen him. How did his name lock into their memory?

Three of us from Community Medical Care — Fred Cooper, a member of the board of directors, Jim Hall, and I — were paying a courtesy call on our new city councilman. "So, how big is your staff?" the councilman asked.

"We're six on the payroll," I said, "with one physician and two family nurse practitioners. We see about 3,500 people a year — children, adults, and seniors." He gave an appreciative whistle, then smiled at Jim. "That's a lot for one doctor, I'd say."

"It would be," I said as tactfully as I knew how, "but in our clinic the two nurses also see patients."

"Oh," he said diplomatically, worried perhaps that his assumption had been politically incorrect. "Got it."

The councilman's assumption was no surprise to me. Any nurse knows how we work almost anonymously, enveloped within the folds of a hospital or community agency. Even though I provide primary health care independently and often alone, I am still "covered" by a physician's name, degree, license, identification numbers, and professional liability policy. But there's more to it than that. Let me give one of my favorite examples of undercover nursing.

It is Wednesday morning, my day off. The phone rings. It's Jim. He's just been beeped, he says, by Minnie Magruder's homemaker, Nora, who says Ms. Minnie is very sick and can hardly get her breath.

She's out of all her medicines and she has no money to buy them. Nora doesn't know what to do — and don't say go to the hospital. She won't. Dr. Hall, please help.

Jim can't make a house call, he says. Can I?

Sure. I call to say I'm coming, stop at the pharmacy for terbutaline, go by the clinic to get some aminophylline, just in case, then drive across town to the senior citizens housing project where Ms. Magruder moved just three weeks ago. She is hunched in her wheelchair, wheezing mightily. I give her the medication and sit down beside her.

Soon, she is able to tell me about the thunderstorm last night that blew in her window and frightened her badly. That's when she started to wheeze, she said. She had a bad night but managed to hold on until Nora arrived. Then the cumulative effects of the move, the storm, the window, the fright, the sleepless night, and the asthma attack came to a head and she broke into the panic that prompted Nora's phone call.

By now, Ms. Magruder is anxious for me to complete my exam. She is looking greedily over my shoulder at the hot dog, fried potatoes, and toast on the kitchen table. Satisfied that she is all right, I get ready to leave. "Phone us again if you need us, okay?" I say. Her mouth is full, but she beams and nods.

As I go out the door, I hear Ms. Magruder and Nora lauding Dr. Hall's efficiency and concern. "Who else would send over your medicine just like that when you need it and can't afford it?" one of them says. I sigh and swear to give Jim the pharmacy bill.

What I should have done is this: I should have stopped in my tracks, turned around, smiled a bright smile and said in a big voice full of surprise, "Dr. Hall, indeed! And who is it standing here in your apartment just like that when you need her?"

Some things never seem to change. There's my collaboration agreement with Jim, signed, dated, and notarized. But Jim still cosigns all my charts for insurance purposes. Third-party billing goes out in his name. As a nurse practitioner, I am authorized to prescribe. But when I phone in a prescription I can bet on the pharmacist saying, "Doctor's name?" after I have given mine. I make referrals. Still, the reports come back, "Dear Dr. Hall...." I do job physicals and sign the report forms. Some come back because "the physician's signature is missing." Sales reps who court me assiduously will not leave samples unless the physician signs for them. Even medical supply houses require a physician's name and Drug Enforcement Administration identification number to open an account.

The social coverage also continues. Every year a Christmas present arrives for Dr. Hall from Dr. Block, a surgeon my colleague Teresa and I "discovered" and refer to. I don't believe Jim has ever sent him a patient. Most astonishing are those patients who, when asked where they go for medical care, say, without missing a beat, "Dr. Hall." Some of them have never seen him. How did his name lock into their memory?

For the sake of argument, let's say I don't mind working undercover. The problem is that this perpetuates the myth that all health care is given under the supervision of physicians, and that physicians are the gatekeepers to all drugs, equipment, supplies, services, and hospitalizations. It means that the health statistics we use are just as erroneous as the 3,500 patients to one doctor assumed by our city councilman. It implies that I don't count as a provider of health care or a decision-maker.

There is at least one thing I can do. I can make sure that all the Minnie Magruders at CMC and all the members of the DC City Council know undercover nursing is archaic. When Ms. Magruder credits her physician for something her nurse has done, I will gently set her straight. And when city officials credit my medical colleague with treating my patients, I will gladly set *them* straight.

This bit of doggerel found its way into an annual
report along with a description of some of our
home care patients who, we all agreed, "should be"
Somewhere Else.

There's a little joke we like to tell
in talk among ourselves
about some people we know well
and a place called Somewhere Else.

Our patients face a sorry plight.
Frail, friendless, insecure,
they've long been hidden out of sight,
anonymous and poor.

When now and then they cause a scene —
they fall and can't get up
or lose their mind or don't keep clean,
the outcry is abrupt.

This person should be Somewhere Else!
They shouldn't be all alone.
So old and sick and in this mess
when we have nursing homes!

But the nursing homes are full, you see
and hospital beds denied,
and home is where they'd rather be —
they know the Lord provides.

So the little joke is really how
we hear the Lord anew
say *Somewhere Else is here for now.*
What I provide is you.

PHOTO: JIM HALL

Alma

After almost thirty years in nursing, half of them at
Community Medical Care, I've run the gamut from novice
to expert. Next time I'm a patient, I'd like to be
taken care of by nurses like me—nurses in their prime.

Sal, my old friend and colleague, has breezed into town for a professional
meeting. We seize the opportunity to get together over dinner and do
some catching up. "So," she says somewhere between the soup and the
salmon, "that's about it for me. I can't believe I'm still at the same job
five years later. I'm usually bored to death after three or four."

"And you?" she asks, settling in to listen. "Last time we talked you
were still working for that clinic— Community Whadya Callit. Ach!
My memory for names is atrocious."

"Yup," I say, "still at Community Medical Care— fourteen years,
same place, same job." I hear myself say this and think I sound apolo-
getic. Am I?

After all, mobility is the norm in nursing. Nurses go from hospital to
hospital, specialty to specialty, degree to degree. We move from clinical
practice to management or education, and sometimes back again. Many of
us leave nursing for other professions. I count among my friends an epi-
demiologist, a minister, a lawyer, a retailer, and an artist— all nurses, once.

What am I still doing at Community Whadya Callit? Am I just plod-
ding along when I ought to look for advancement, new challenges, more
education, or, at least, more money? Why am I not "bored to death?"

I think about the Board of Nursing examiner who paid an
official visit to a community college where I was helping to develop the
nursing curriculum. In spirited defense of a disputed state licensure
requirement that all nurses complete so many hours of this and so many
of that, she drew herself up to a truly modest height and proclaimed,

"Why, I've given over a thousand enemas in my career and I can tell you this: I learned from every one of them!"

I had my doubts then. I have them now. In any case, I've already done "so many hours" of just about everything in my field: primary health care. I remember the first chance I had to do a pelvic exam at CMC. The patient was a thirty-year-old Peruvian primagravida, as nervous as I was. Jim, my physician colleague, was encouraging. "Go ahead," he said. "I'll be your assistant." I thought it over, then pulled Jim out of the room for a quick conference. "The thing is this," I told him honestly. "I can't put in a speculum and speak Spanish at the same time."

Then there was the first day I worked alone in the office. Quaking behind what I hoped was an "I can handle anything" façade, I faced enormities like the painful, bulging hemorrhoid plaguing my first patient. I am sure I lavished the same attention on it that a vascular surgeon would on a bulging aortic aneurysm.

That was at the beginning. Within a few years I was taking pelvises and hemorrhoids in stride.

And now? Now I can walk with an unshakable calm into a room full of squalling toddlers, talk easily above the din with whoever brought them to the clinic, and sort out their complaints as I examine whatever part of whichever child presents itself to me. With confidence in my clinical judgment and my cross-cultural skills, I can work with a sixty-year-old Salvadoran woman who longs only for home but is unlikely to get there if her dangerously high blood glucose is not controlled. "I know the pills are not working," she says matter-of-factly, "but I will not take the shots. The shots killed my sister."

Now, I can look at a Gram stain under the microscope and identify just about every red and blue form I find there. I can spend a few minutes with someone and get a pretty good idea of how sick or well they are. I can diagnose without fear. And I never have to rewrite my chart notes for clarity. (Well, almost never.)

I feel I've run the gamut from novice to expert. And it's a good feeling — something like a runner's high. Well worth the cost in time, effort, and conditioning.

As I write this, I wonder how many of America's two million nurses are giving hands-on care. And I wonder how many of those feel like I do. It's hard if you drop in and out of nursing or work only part-time. It's hard if your primary job is teaching, managing, planning, or any one of the many important but non-clinical jobs nurses do. It's nearly impossible if you are distracted by unsatisfactory working conditions or the expectation that, no matter what you are doing and no matter how good you are at doing it, you'll eventually move on to something else.

Frankly, I wonder if there are enough of us to go around. Why? Because the next time I'm a patient, I'd really like to be taken care of by nurses like me — nurses who know they're in their prime.

One of my favorite illustrations from the "What Do Nurses Do?" coloring book (see page 205)

"Are you a doctor or a nurse?" Sabrina asks. "I never did know for sure." "I'm a nurse," I say brightly, hoping my answer will satisfy her.

As a child, I was haunted by a Bible verse that went like this: "Be ready at all times to answer anyone who asks you why you believe as you do" (1 Peter 3:15). I understood it as a commandment equal to the first ten and with the same dire consequences for failure to perform. Drawing from the illustrations I had seen in Bible storybooks, I would imagine myself in a huge palace or amphitheater standing alone at the bottom of a wide marble staircase looking up at the remote but imposing figure on the dais (maybe an emperor) who would decide my fate. "WELL?" his voice would come thundering down, "WHAT IS YOUR ANSWER?" And, in my imagination, it was never good enough, strong enough, clear enough. I was often sent to the lions.

In my adult life, the commandment still haunts me and the voices still come thundering down, but the questioners these days seem less interested in my religious beliefs than in my beliefs about my profession. No, there are no palaces or emperors. What happens is something like this: I have just left the clinic where I work, heading home, when I see Sabrina, a young mother with a baby, bottle, tote bag, and purse on one arm, trying to hail a cab with the other. Both she and her baby are my patients. "Where are you headed, Sabrina?" I call to her. "Can I give you a ride?" She is more than happy to pile into my car and we drive off, chatting about the high cost of babies and cab fare.

About ten minutes into our journey, Sabrina gets quiet for a moment, then changes the subject: "Are you a doctor or a nurse?" she asks. "I never did know for sure."

I've told her. Told her more than once. Why doesn't she—how could she possibly not—know? I am distressed, but don't want to overreact. "A nurse," I say simply, brightly, hoping that's it for today.

"Well then, what's the difference between being a doctor and a nurse?" she asks in a voice that sounds suddenly like thunder rolling down.

Can't she see? Isn't it clear—the difference between physicians and nurses? Apparently not. Not to Sabrina, not to the general public, not even to many of my colleagues in the health professions with whom I've discussed it. Sure, there are plenty of assumptions, mostly wrong but sprung from a kernel of truth:

The physician is a man; the nurse is a woman.

A physician has lots of education; a nurse has less.

A physician wears a lab coat; a nurse wears a white uniform and cap.

A physician writes prescriptions; a nurse takes orders.

The physician is cold and aloof; the nurse is warm and caring.

A physician is rich; a nurse isn't.

Sabrina knows there is more to it than this. What she doesn't know is that nurse theoreticians have spent entire careers trying to answer her simple question, and that even I, an everyday practicing nurse who has had to answer it hundreds of times, am still afraid that my answer will not be good enough, strong enough, clear enough to suit her.

It is not that I don't have an answer, but it is framed in terms intended for me and my fellow nurses. In my view, nursing and medicine are two ways of healing that usually work in tandem but can be defined separately. Medicine is healing in the masculine mode, characteristically logical, technological, prescriptive. Nursing is healing in the feminine mode: intuitive, personal, integrative. To colleagues who object to my use of masculine and feminine, I say medicine is the diagnosis and treatment of disease while nursing is healing through care and nurture. A given doctor or nurse (a good one, anyway) both doctors and nurses, but functions most effectively in his or her primary practice mode.

I think of how my friend Jean describes what she calls medical and nursing styles among her colleagues in the special care nursery where she works. According to Jean, when a ventilated premie's oxygen monitor alarm goes off, the high-tech nurse in neonatal intensive care's first move is usually to work the machinery. "I prefer the nursing style," Jean says. "I take my time—let the alarm run for a little bit, and watch the baby to see what's happening. I may change its position, make it more comfortable, or reduce environmental stimuli. Only if these measures fail do I adjust the oxygen setting on the ventilator."

To Sabrina, I say, "I don't want to oversimplify, but a doctor who sees you as a patient is likely to be thinking, 'What's the problem here?' A nurse is more likely to be thinking, 'How is she feeling?' The doctor wants to diagnose your disease and treat it. The nurse wants to help you feel better."

Sabrina doesn't respond right away. Is she confused, satisfied, or just ready to change the subject again? "So you're a nurse," she says at last. "I was just wondering. It doesn't really matter though."

"TO THE LIONS!" booms a voice in my head, rolling down like thunder.

Interesting, this mindset: You want comprehensive, high-quality, cost-effective, and personalized care for the poor—so you need more doctors. And yet, here I am giving just this kind of care to just these people. Only I am a nurse.

It's Saturday morning and I am sitting in the living room with a cup of coffee and a week's worth of news clippings delivered by my personal clipping service, CMC volunteer Vern Renshaw. One from the front page of the *New York Times* catches my eye.[20] It covers Mayor Dinkins's plan to open twenty new health centers in New York City that will provide the poor with comprehensive health care and, what's more, their own private doctor. The principal motivation is financial: to reduce rising Medicaid costs for emergency room visits and hospitalizations that could be avoided by means of well-organized and personalized primary health care services. Even so, I have to admit I am touched by Deputy Mayor Cesar Perales's statement that "all children deserve a doctor who knows their name."

Yes, I think to myself, healing often hangs on something as simple as names: whose name you know and who knows yours. I read on. Bad news. Some health officials believe the mayor's recipe may fail for want of one ingredient: doctors. Dr. Kenneth E. Raske of the Greater New York Hospital Association is quoted as saying, "The main ingredient to make this proposal work is doctors, and I don't know where we are going to get them because we are not training the right type of doctors who want to do good will in the world and not just earn a lot of money."

Interesting, this mindset. Not just Dr. Raske's. Practically everyone's. You want comprehensive, high-quality, cost-effective, and person-

alized care for the poor? You need
doctors. And yet here I am, giving
just this kind of care to just these people
in a city not so different from New York.
Only I am a nurse — one of many thousands of
nurses with special training in primary health care.
I guess nobody sees us. It's as if the people of a town were
convinced they were going to starve for want of meat.
"We have no poultry, no beef or pork, not even any game," they cry
pitifully. "Our children will die." And not one of them sees the lake
at the edge of town, jumping with fish.

I lean back in my chair and imagine how New York might react to
the news that nurse practitioners could serve in lieu of the revered but
elusive "old-fashioned family doctor" in these inner-city clinics. I suspect most would be dubious. The mayor might say, "But we don't want
second-class medical care for the poor. The poor of this city deserve
the best we can offer." The holders of the purse strings might say, "Oh
no you don't. It's hard enough paying the doctors. If we let a whole
other group of health care providers start dipping into the till, it'll be
empty quicker than you can say CAT scan."

If I am not mistaken, the administrators, doctors, and lawyers
would sing the same song in three-part harmony.

The administrators: "Nurses are great, but they need to work
under the supervision of doctors. We would simply be adding another
layer of bureaucracy."

The doctors: "Nurses haven't had a medical education. They
might not recognize the difference between an ordinary whatchamacallit
and a dangerous thingamabob."

The lawyers: "Nurses would be practicing medicine without a
license. We'd be wide open to lawsuits."

The people? I only know how first-time callers to my clinic

respond when asked whether they object to being scheduled with the nurse instead of the doctor. "I don't mind," they say, "as long as she can write prescriptions." Once established as patients, they seem well satisfied with their care and unconcerned about having a doctor who is really a nurse.

And nurses. What do nurses say? Some argue that what I do isn't really nursing, that meat is meat and fish is fish and that the two cannot serve the same purpose. So even we nurses have to open our minds, question our assumptions, and get a fresh perspective once in a while.

Do nurses give second-class primary health care?

Are the majority of human ailments best treated by a practitioner with a traditional medical education?

In the real world, do physicians give top priority to preventive health services?

Must a primary health care provider cost $100,000 per year?

Should our laws continue to restrict the practice of "the healing art" to physicians?

I skim the article again. No. No mention of nurses. Too bad, because I believe that all people deserve to have a nurse who knows their name.

Like keys on a ring, I carry with me a set of simple phrases that flash through my mind even at the busiest times. Each of them opens a way for me to get in touch with what I hold most important in nursing practice. I pass them on to the 1992 graduates of the nurse practitioner program at the University of Virginia.

No doubt about it. Nursing used to be a whole lot simpler. I remember my first day as a nursing student. There was a large, tiered classroom. Down in front, on the dais, was a hospital bed and an instructor dressed in white. That first day in Fundamentals of Nursing we were taught how to make a bed and give a bed bath. From the beginning, nursing proved to be just what I imagined: taking care of sick people with skill and compassion.

Thirty years later, I find nursing much more complicated. The profession has been fairly bombarded with theories, models, and frameworks that purport to explain and order what nurses do. There are specialties, roles, and practice settings I never heard of as a neophyte, complex legalities that I never had to reckon with. There is a vast health sciences literature that includes dozens of nursing journals and who knows how many texts and videos, plus the thousands of continuing education programs offered each year. National and local politics directly influence my own practice, as do the realities of the place where I work, the people I work with, and those I take care of.

What does it all come down to? How do I key into nursing day to day? One thing that has helped is a set of simple phrases or cues that flash through my mind even at the busiest times. I think of them as keys on a ring because each of them opens a way for me to get in touch with what I hold most important in nursing practice.

Recently I counted them. There were seven.

The first and most important is: I am a healer. That means my job is not just to make a diagnosis, perform a procedure, or even to establish a therapeutic relationship with a patient, although it may include these. It is to do all in my power to promote or restore a sense of health and well-being within that person. Healing can happen in the presence of disease, in spite of mistakes, and with access to only the most basic resources. Healing is a power I possess in some measure and I have committed myself to using it effectively and responsibly.

The next is: Who's in charge? I sometimes picture decision-making as a giant beach ball lobbed back and forth between patient and nurse. "I can make recommendations but the final decision is yours," I say, tossing the ball. To which the patient responds, "Please, tell me what to do," and sends it back to me. Sometimes I realize I've been holding the ball too long—or, worse, have run away with it altogether. When I am properly keyed in, I can sense when to toss the ball and when to catch it.

The big picture. Am I seeing it? Here sits a young man with stomach pain. Can I enlarge my focus to include the background? Ah, a sixteen-year-old high school dropout whose girlfriend is about to give birth to his child and whose mother has just kicked him out of the house. The big picture sometimes changes everything.

What besides pills? In our culture, there is a tremendous demand for pills and, in the medical profession, tremendous pressure to prescribe them. But I am a nurse. I see that my sixteen-year-old with stomach pain needs more than pills. A listening ear, touch maybe, information certainly, support, an environment in which healing can take place.

Count the cost. Baseline bloodwork costs $30. An upper-GI series costs $330. Thirty Zantac tablets cost $47. Plus the cost of office visits.

My patient has a part-time job at McDonald's. He has no health insurance. He can't afford "the best." The gold standard is beyond our reach,
but first-class second-class care is not.

From somewhere in the turbulence of my mind as I try to devise
a plan for my sick young patient, a single thought rises to the surface:
prevention. Should I ask an acutely ill, homeless father-to-be what
he is doing to protect himself against sexually transmitted diseases?
Surely not now. But if not now, when? As soon as he feels better, he'll
stop coming. A nurse's conscience is implacable. Prevention.
Count the cost.

Finally: For a true healer, one who is willing to see patients in context, relinquish control, consider a wide range of therapeutic options,
count the costs, and think prevention, there is no such thing
as routine. The concept is antithetical to nursing. It's never
"just" a blood pressure check, just a prescription refill, just a pregnancy
test, just a shot, just a job physical— and certainly never just a kid with
a stomachache.

Writing prescriptions, I've always believed, could easily become the centerpiece of my work as a nurse practitioner just as passing meds used to seem like my main job when I worked as team leader on a hospital ward.

"Teresa!" I yell from the front door of the clinic after signing my name on the UPS delivery man's clipboard. "Our order from the printer is here!" Teresa, my colleague at Community Medical Care, puts down her pen, leaves the stack of charts on her desk, and joins me for the grand opening.

It's been a long time coming, this order from the printer. Years, in fact. It started with the passage of the District of Columbia's Health Occupations Revision Act in 1986 and the sentence that began, "The advanced registered nurse may perform actions of medical diagnosis, treatment, and prescription...." But the act and the sentence carried no weight until publication of the rules and regulations that interpreted them, two years later in 1988. And the rules and regulations meant nothing until the first advanced practice RN licenses were issued in 1991.

Now, in 1992, the culmination of the whole process was about to take place. We tore off the paper and opened the box. There they were. Two thousand prescription blanks with three names rather than one at the top. As holder of prescriptive authority, James L. Hall, MD, had just been joined by Veneta Masson, RN, and Teresa Acquaviva, RN.

Of course, it took a little time to get used to signing our own names on prescriptions. I slipped once in a while and wrote "James L. Hall" just as I had been doing for the past thirteen years. But I'd tear up the scrip with a rueful shrug and start over. Granted, there were pharmacists who made a point of telling us we could not prescribe (patently false) or that the pharmacy law did not include nurses as a category of health professional on whose authority drugs could be dispensed (alas, true).

Still, our written scrips have seldom been refused and, about one time in ten, my phoned prescriptions are accepted without the query, "Doctor's name?" at the end. Most important, new patients no longer take their prescriptions, look them over, then say to me, "Thanks, Dr. Hall."

It's a new age all right, yet, despite the fact that I require prescriptive authority to function effectively in my primary health care setting, I'm ambivalent about having received it. Writing prescriptions, I've always believed, could easily become the centerpiece of my work just as passing meds used to seem like my main job when I worked as team leader on a hospital ward. Many of my patients expect a prescription for every symptom. Not only do I find myself caving in to their demands, I confess to prescribing as a means of moving lengthy patient encounters along. For your ear? Use these drops. For your back, take this. Your stomach, your rash, your insomnia? Try this and this and this. I do it more than I used to.

Years ago, when a new patient would come in for birth control, I never made assumptions about what she wanted. I'd spend time discussing the options, then ask her which she thought would be best for her. Over time I learned that it was almost always the pill. Now I don't waste time on prologue. When a woman says birth control, I say,

COMMUNITY MEDICAL CARE
JAMES L. HALL, M.D.
VENETA MASSON, R.N., F.N.P.
TERESA ACQUAVIVA, R.N., F.N.P.

1118 NINTH STREET, N.W.   WASHINGTON, D. C. 20001

_____ AGE _____

NAME _____

_____ DATE _____

ADDRESS _____

R̸

"The pill?" The other day I was taken aback when a thirty-year-old Hispanic woman actually said, "No. You see, I'm on the pill now and it's causing these brown spots on my face. A friend of mine said I should try the diaphragm—it works really well for her. But when I went to the clinic at the hospital, the doctor told me, 'Well, what we have here is the pill. Take it or leave it.' He said it in a nice way but that's what he said." I was appalled. Then my eyes moved inexorably to my watch. How much time would it take me to teach an inexperienced, non-English-speaking woman what she needed to know about diaphragms? Answer: more than I had.

Like the vast majority of my patients, I believe in the importance of drugs to modern health care—even to holistic health care. But that doesn't keep me from fantasizing about how my job would be different (better?) if I told patients, "I don't prescribe medications, but I really think I can help you with that low back pain. Let's talk about body mechanics, strengthening exercises, heat and rest, maybe even a diet to lose some of those pounds you've gained over the last few years." It would take me a lot more time, but then I'd have more, because my patients would be running away in droves.

I realize that rejecting prescriptive authority on the grounds that it distracts my attention from the big picture is not a desirable option. My challenge is clear and simple: Don't substitute pills for the patience, care, and skill it takes to nurse.

As a health care provider, I shouldn't be pushed to the limit simply trying to do my job. The hardness, bitterness, and cynicism I feel—don't they make me just one more symptom of a sick system when I could be part of the cure?

In 1993, Community Medical Care and I celebrate our fifteenth year on Ninth Street. Odd that this year, for the first time, my batteries have gone dead. In the past, I've always been able to recharge them. Not now. I haven't exactly winked out like an old-fashioned otoscope during otitis season. I'm just overcome by an intense desire to retreat to my fantasy apartment in Cairo overlooking the Nile where I daydream, write, and entertain a select circle of artists and cosmopolites. I used to jet there after work from time to time, or on weekends after a rough week. Now, it's all I can do to come back to another day in this dreary Washington neighborhood within spitting distance of the Capitol.

I don't think Laverne's hitting me up for money twice in two weeks was what made me short out. It's more than just Laverne. I've known her and the members of her vast extended family for all of my fifteen years at the clinic. They come when they are sick or hurting—or when the school or welfare office requires information about someone's health status. She'd been in a couple of months ago to try again for a tubal ligation. She didn't want the baby she was about to have. She hadn't wanted any of the last several, but Medicaid no longer pays for abortions and you have to sign the consent for a ligation sixty days in advance of the procedure.

Sharon, as patient care coordinator and mother hen, had helped her get the necessary papers. But Laverne didn't know when she was due—

hadn't had any prenatal care this time either, despite the fact that we've always been there for her whether or not she had an appointment.

Sure, we're motivated by her need, but also by the $45.30 we get for a Medicaid visit. She is dependent on us and we, as a struggling non-profit organization, need every $45.30 we can collect. I resent this kind of mutual dependency. I am angry that, because she delivered before the sixty days were up, she had to leave the hospital without getting her tubes tied. I bristle at being pressed for cash to buy milk and Pampers when I know how much drug money passes in and out of her house: a lot more than there is in the clinic's bank account.

"I'll help you out today," I tell her, stroking the baby's cheek, "but this is the last time." And I mean it. I feel hard as a stone.

You'd think I'd feel better about Rosario. She has no expectations. As an undocumented alien, she has no entitlements to anything except prenatal care at government clinics. For well-child care and her own, she pays us $20 a visit, not all at once, but *poco a poco* with what she earns from her "part-time" cleaning offices at night. But now she needs more than what we can provide. She's been bleeding for over two months. Nothing that couldn't be cured with a simple D&C, but nothing is simple for Rosario. We sent her to DC General—the only place that would even let her in the door—with a referral explaining how the medicines had failed, how her hemoglobin had already dropped from 13 to 9. They sent her home with an application for the Medical Charities program that will take forty-five days to process after documentation is complete. I feel drained by Rosario's need. I hate telling her she can't just offer to pay the hospital *poco a poco*. I can't find a good way to explain why, in such a rich country, with the necessary technology at hand, she must continue to hemorrhage. Taking care of Rosario, I feel bitter as gall.

It is not always better for those who have money and health insurance. When my friend Faye went to a doctor complaining of elbow pain that got worse with movement, she found herself a candidate for coronary bypass surgery despite the fact that antianginal medications didn't relieve her pain and her cardiac workup demonstrated no pathology. Listening to Faye's story, I feel cynical as a sneer. I've been told the same thing she was: Don't worry, I know what's best for you. Don't worry, your insurance will cover it.

I've never claimed that health care was a right. I acknowledge the profound social and political challenges posed by the entrenched underclass, the flood of illegal immigrants from third world countries, and the brazenness and greed inherent in our health care system. But I've come to believe that despite these, given the will to do so, we can provide decent and affordable basic health care to everyone. I, as a health care provider, shouldn't have to be pushed to the limit simply trying to do my job. My needs as a patient shouldn't be defined by my health insurance coverage.

This hardness, bitterness, and cynicism I feel—don't they make me just one more symptom of a sick system when I could be part of the cure?

What balm is there in this violent Gilead to make the wounded whole? This question came to me over and over during the years I worked at Community Medical Care. Although we at the clinic were deeply committed to the health of the people of our neighborhood, it became clear to us that many of the causes of their suffering were beyond our capacity to heal.

Sunday
after church
under a sleeve of summer sky
we walk up the alley
called Wiltberger Street
look down
at the blood-stained cement.

He was fourteen
on just another
hip hop high top
Saturday
in the hood when
somebody put his lights out—
semiautomatic.

The people who live
on the alley
behind brick façades
won't talk
but lock up their kids

for the weekend.
They could be next.

I want to kneel
in this stagnant pool
of spent rage,
smear the blood all over
my face, my clothes
and wander like Cain
through the city and say

> *Look at me and see*
> *what I have seen.*

But I don't.
I stay where I am,
nursing the wounds
that never heal for want
of the capacity to feel—
like ulcers on a sole
bereft of sensation.

What balm is there
in this violent Gilead
to make the wounded whole?
I know no cure
and all I have is breath
a voice
and memory—

> a memory
> a voice.

I don't have a grand plan for health care reform. What I have to offer is more like a little notebook of small ideas that I think could save lots of money and improve health care.

These days I can't seem to read a newspaper, listen to a talk show, attend a conference, or converse with a colleague without the subject of national health care reform coming up. Everyone has either a plan or an opinion about someone else's. In the course of debating them, catchy terms like pay-or-play, managed competition, and single-party payer get strewn about like so many half-empty glasses at a cocktail party.

I've been thinking that, since none of the existing plans seems to me both attractive and workable, I should come up with my own. But I don't have a broad enough perspective on the problems and potential solutions. I only know what works for me —a nurse in a small clinic at the tip of the massive upside-down pyramid we call the American health care system. At Community Medical Care, we encounter all the health care needs experienced by most Americans and do most of the things health care providers in this country do (do them well, I might add), but with less money and fewer resources because the patients we see are mostly poor and uninsured.

Markus, weighing in

I'm afraid I can't come up with a Plan. What I have to offer is more like a little notebook of small ideas that I like to think could save lots of money and improve health care if implemented on a large scale.

Let me share a few of them with you.

First: Start low, go slow. This old aphorism has been passed down to generations of students learning how to prescribe medications. You start with the lowest dose and increase it slowly until you achieve a therapeutic effect. This way, you avoid overdosing and treating in excess of need. The patient is spared unnecessary side effects. A simple idea. A good one, too. Why don't we apply it more broadly? In primary health care, why not use nurses (who cost less and often have a better grasp of the context in which health problems have arisen) before physicians, and generalists before specialists? Why not consider watchful waiting rather than aggressive treatment in situations where a medical problem is likely to resolve itself spontaneously? Why not use low tech before high tech, home care before hospital admission? At CMC, we have to practice this way, but I notice that, most of the time, it works very well.

Hold on to those baby books. You know, the ones that record your baby's growth, developmental milestones, illnesses, immunizations. Because our patients, like most, are likely to pop up at various places in the health care system, we believe in keeping those baby books up to date and encouraging mothers to take them to every medical appointment they make for their child. We also give what we call a prenatal passbook to each pregnant woman that contains vital information about the course of her pregnancy, lab test results, special problems, and whom to contact for help in an emergency. What if everyone had custody of their lifetime health records and could present them when they showed up at a new medical facility or switched to a new health plan? I think of the time and money that could be saved at our clinic alone on reconstructing medical histories, requesting and responding to requests for medical records, repeating tests, prescribing previously tried, ineffective treatments, and making mistakes based on incomplete or erroneous recollections.

Get personal. Last week a patient told me, "Yeah, we have an HMO now, but we just use it for emergencies. You see a different person every time and besides, our insurance is going to be changed at the end of the year anyhow. This is where I come and this is where I bring my baby."

At CMC, we're small and personal. We also have a secret ingredient. Her name is Sharon and she has occupied a red leather swivel armchair at the front desk for fifteen years now. She's accessible by phone and by opening the front door. She's from the community, knows every resource in it, and has authority within the organization. With patients, she can praise or chide—and she will stop everything to listen to what a person has to say. She bends the rules or enforces them, whatever is called for, and she acts as interpreter between patients and staff. Sharon tells me what to do and, often enough, how to do it. Seed the system with Sharons and all America would know how to use their health plan and how to gain access to community resources. They would understand what the doctor was trying to say, how to do what has to be done, and where to go when all else fails.

At Community Medical Care, we've had a taste of managed care. It snuck up on us a few years ago in the form of the Sugarplum Health Plan for Medicaid recipients. We've learned that a plan that sounds good on paper and in your living room may not work well in practice.

Where I work, we've had a taste of health care reform. Where I work is a small, private nonprofit clinic in inner-city Washington, DC, and what we've had a taste of is managed care for Medicaid recipients. It snuck up on us a few years ago in the form of the Sugarplum Health Plan (not, of course, its real name). All through the poor neighborhoods surrounding our clinic, we began to see billboards and buses advertising Sugarplum — just the name, an appealing logo, and a phone number. Television ads showed a kindly doctor picking up the phone to counsel a worried patient. "Yes," he says, "let's get you in here to see me today!"

Up and down the streets women with children in tow were approached by neighborly recruiters. "Do you have Medicaid? May I have just a minute of your time?" And in school, children learned about Sugarplum. The ones who came back with the greatest number of completed application forms would win a free pizza. "Please, Mom — Please, Ms. Sallie — Please, Aunt Dorothy — just sign this paper so I can get a free pizza. Please?"

I don't know what the Sugarplum street workers promised their prospects, but I know what our patients heard: "Turn in your Medicaid card, and join a brand new health insurance plan that offers a whole lot more. You'll have a private doctor. You don't want to change? Sure, you can keep the one you already have. We'll provide transportation to and from your appointments. And you won't even have to pay the fifty cents for your prescriptions. They'll all be free."

Many of our patients signed on. Who wouldn't? There was only one problem. The recruitment campaign was far better organized and held more promise than the health plan itself. As it turned out, you couldn't keep your own doctor unless he or she was one of the very few on the Sugarplum provider panel. Not only that, the new Sugarplum policyholders had no idea how the plan worked—how to sign up with a doctor, for example, and why you couldn't just show up at the emergency room anymore without preauthorization. What's preauthorization? And where are those street workers now that we have questions?

Getting off the Sugarplum Plan and back on regular Medicaid proved difficult. No one in authority was particularly eager to help, and the penalty for succeeding was a month or more without any coverage at all. So, our erstwhile patients simply continued to show up in our office, expecting to be seen as usual. They had no intention of paying for the clinic services they had always received free. Reimbursement became our problem, not theirs. If little Tamika was sick, were we going to turn her away—little Tamika whose mother had been our patient when *she* was a child? No, these are the ties that bind.

We've learned some lessons from our experience with the Sugarplum Health Plan. The first is that health care reform is coming, regardless of what federal legislation is eventually passed, and that managed care will be a part of it.

The second is that a plan that looks good on paper and sounds good in your living room may not work well in practice. Especially if you're poor, can't read, don't know what questions to ask, and aren't in a position to plan ahead because you lurch from one crisis to the next, and it's all you can do to make it through one day at a time, even in the best of times.

Sugarplum was right on target in its advertising campaign and its use of street workers to sign people up. It was correct in its assumption that poor people, like almost everyone else, prefer to have a "private doctor." It understood that lack of transportation is a major barrier to the use of health services (why else are there so many ambulance calls from poor neighborhoods?), as are copayments, even the fifty cents adults must pay for each Medicaid prescription. But Sugarplum was wrong in assuming that people who have grown up with a certain pattern of health-seeking behavior can change it without a great deal of support. Those street recruiters should also serve as local information booths, teaching people one to one, neighbor to neighbor, how to get what they're entitled to.

President Clinton's *Health Security Act* promises to integrate Medicaid beneficiaries into the new system. If our experience with the Sugarplum Health Plan is any indication, this will be easier said than done. Those people born into poverty who make up what economists call the underclass aren't used to paying for health or social services. They figure that a clinic like ours gets a government check, just like they do. What costs money and they can live without, they do without. Health is not a high priority. So much for the idea of copayments.

Other groups of poor people, such as the growing number of Central American immigrants moving into the clinic neighborhood, know full well that they are entitled to nothing. Health care reform will not change that fact. They are willing to pay fees for service but can only manage it *poco a poco*. They wait for a crisis before incurring what, in terms of their income, seem like huge bills, even if those charges represent a small fraction of the cost of the care. And they avoid large institutions where they cannot make themselves understood and where they believe they risk attracting unwanted attention to their immigrant status. So much for universal coverage.

Health organizations that exist to care for people living on the fringes of society due to poverty, language, culture, or lifestyle know the importance of personality. Just because you open your doors doesn't mean throngs of sufferers will immediately surge through them. What counts is the word on the street and your consistent attention to the faces, names, needs, and expectations of your clientele over time—a good long time. Whether you succeed in building trust depends on how flexible your policies are, where you're located, what the place looks and feels like, how patient and tuned-in the staff is, and how patients feel they've been treated.

Small, personal organizations are usually more effective in serving minority populations than large, complicated ones. But with health care reform, the survival of small, independent clinics like ours is in jeopardy. Either we will be swallowed up into health alliances that will determine what we do and how we do it or we will remain dependent on contributions from individuals, churches, and foundations that wonder why, what with health care for all, we still ask them for money.

One thing I know for sure: health workers and insurers aren't exactly queuing up to serve the poor, so it's not likely anyone will be there to take our place if we go under. Most important is that a Health Security card from the U.S. government cannot guarantee anyone, rich or poor, the benefits of the art of healing. The most it can provide is a package of services, procedures, and treatments that represent applications of the science of medicine.

Unless nurses and doctors continue to learn and practice the healing art—for which there is no procedure code, no reimbursement, no real appreciation among bureaucrats and politicians, and precious little time in an increasingly regimented health care system—only a fortunate few will be able to obtain this therapy that money cannot buy. I hope my patients will always be among them.

With attention to showmanship, costume, choreography, props and stage sets, the artful nurse is a walking, talking tonic.

Think about it — isn't it just so? Here I am, singing the Barney song to a fearful child as I playfully advance the dreaded otoscope toward the ear in which I have told him I'm going to look for Barney. "I love you, you love me, we're a happy family…" And, miraculously, the child sits motionless in his mother's arms while I sing and look and say with almost genuine regret, "You know, Barney's not there, just a bright red eardrum. Maybe he's in the other ear. Let's look and see." The child turns his head and offers me the other ear.

Amazing, the power of a tall, purple dinosaur from a popular kids' show to calm a terrified toddler. Or is it the song? Or the singing? Amazing, too, at least to me, was hearing at a recent nursing conference how several of my colleagues have adopted the same technique. How did we, working on our own, make the discovery that Barney hides in ears and, given that, realize we now had the means to ally ourselves and our otoscopes with children who are skeptical, but willing to entertain the possibility that it's true? I suppose it's the same as with other momentous discoveries — theories arise, are investigated and then reported independently by solitary researchers from more than one remote outpost.

But I don't want you to get the impression that my talents are limited to a rendition of the Barney song. In fact, my pediatric repertoire has expanded considerably through the years. My audience also likes the song "This Little Light of Mine" to accompany the bouncing ophthalmoscope or the flashing otoscope (which, at the end, they blow out like a birthday candle). I get requests for "Peek-a-boo" from my younger audience and "Let's Pretend" from the older ones. Parents seem to like to play "You're not going to believe this but…" after I toss them an opener like, "What has little Spike done to surprise you lately?" After listening attentively, my next volley always includes at least one synonym of "marvelous" and an appreciative chuckle or awed silence. I've got my part down pat though I'll often change the delivery on a whim.

Nursing adults requires artistry of a different order. It is more subtle, more demanding, rather like improvisation. With adults, I have to play different characters at different times. Sometimes my patient assigns me a particular role, for example, the authoritarian: "I don't want to hear any more. You're supposed to tell me what to do," Miss Louise said one day, overwhelmed by all the either-ors I was offering her. Other times, I choose my own role— colleague, mother, sister, aunt.

Performing with the kids

"Here's the report," I might say. "What do you think?" Or, with another person in another situation, "Look, we go back a long way together. I know a lot of what you've been through. It's not so easy to tell you this, but…" How do I know which fits? Experience, intuition, and coaching by experts through the years.

Of course, there's more to performance art than words and song. Costume, for example. For nurses, it's usually a choice between uniform or street clothes—although there's a wide latitude for self expression within each category. You can be the executive in the tailored three-piece suit or the eat-my-dust nurse on the run in scrubs, the starched and all-but-capped Big Nurse or the Hip Sistah in dangly earrings and dashiki at the teen clinic.

So what makes for star quality among nurse artists? There's choreography: how we move, the vibes we send, our use of space, touch. And props: the equipment hanging out of every cloth orifice, the flower on the desk, the beeper going off every five minutes just like a snooze alarm, the needle cap between the teeth, the pins, badges, buttons, and slogans affixed to our garments. And, of course, stage sets: the bare, minimalist cubicle, the noisy, high-tech white space littered with people and things in perpetual random motion, the street, the factory, the school, church, home.

So what makes for star quality among nurse artists? All of us get training and acquire experience. We can choose the place in which to showcase our talent. I'd say that knowing the audience, being a quick study, and playing from the heart separate the good from the mediocre. Then there's skill—the kind you work long and hard to perfect until the injections never hurt, the dressing just looks and feels right every time, the advice is always practical and timely. The artful nurse is a walking, talking tonic.

But star quality? Who can say? We just know it when we see it—like Barney.

Over the years, the clinic staff assembled a unique collection of carols that we sang with gusto and, often, hilarity at the annual Christmas party. Each was set to a familiar tune. Although the songs often contained insider jokes and references to memorable events (you had to've been there!), this one by Teresa just might appeal to a broader audience.

(to the tune "What Child Is This?")

1. Whose child is this that's underfoot,
    Who squirms about and won't stay put?
    Where is the mom? Where is the dad?
    Who comes today with this sick lad?

Refrain

    This, this is well child care,
    It drives you nuts and makes you swear,
    Colds, flu, and DPTs
    MMRs and PPDs.

2. You schedule one, but then bring three.
    What can we do? You're family.
    One's in the room, one's in the lab
    And mom's at the liquor store, buying a Tab.

3. We've talked and looked and now it's time
    To draw your blood and do the Tine.
    You look with fear and then you scream.
    We have to call the blood-drawing team.

4. And now we're done, O little one.
    A sticker for your bravery!
    You're free to go, but we must stay.
    The paperwork will take all day.

Kevin making a joyful noise

My nurse colleagues and I are always preoccupied with the contents of our personal skill bank. We collect new skills like shiny new coins and work hard to keep the ones we already own polished to perfection. Technology only feeds our craving for more.

There's this word that caught my eye as I sifted through the pages of a nursing journal that landed on my desk: multiskilling. It appeared in an article that also featured the words downsizing and restructuring. The gist of the piece seemed to be that life for health professionals is getting tough and uncertain (see "downsizing" and "restructuring"), so we had better be prepared for anything (see "multiskilling").

Yes, skills are (and always have been) vital to nursing—a source of pride and identity to the practitioner, a source of comfort and most important, healing, to the patient. My colleagues and I are always preoccupied with the contents of our personal skill bank. We watch each other in action out of the corner of one eye, grading a performance or looking for tips on how to improve our own. We rate nursing programs in terms of the skill level its graduates achieve. We collect new skills like shiny new coins and work hard to keep the ones we already own polished to perfection.

I still remember my principal regret about leaving a part-time job in urgent care that really didn't suit me. I'd just learned how to sew (people, not clothing), and since completing one intensive workshop on suturing, I'd actually done it only five times—hardly enough to feel sure of myself. I knew if I didn't continue to use it, I'd lose it. Simple as that. I felt the same way about giving up venipuncture, even after years of daily practice. Sure it saves me time and the lab tech can do it just as well (maybe), but it felt like losing precious capital from my professional brokerage account.

"I like to pick up new skills every year or so," my colleague Lou said. She'd just mastered endometrial biopsy and was setting her sights on learning colposcopy. "I know what you mean," said Jeannette, flushed with pride at having received her certificate in sigmoidoscopy. Ah, technology! How it feeds our skill addiction, our craving for more. Surely it has shaped our definition of the skilled nurse.

But skilled nurses are more than the sum of the procedures they perform. Of course. They're smart, up-to-date and can apply what they know. I still recall a coworker's simple but eloquent compliment when I found a small thyroid nodule in the course of a routine exam of a healthy adolescent. "Good pick-up," he said. I was pleased with myself and spent the rest of the day fingering the figurative gold coin in my pocket that signifies smarts.

So, anything else that contributes to skill? Yes, as a matter of fact. It's art. One of the dictionary definitions of art is "a specific skill in adept performance, conceived as requiring the exercise of intuitive faculties that cannot be learned solely by study," as in the art of writing letters. Just so the art of nursing.

Think for a moment of all the ways you've heard the following announcement: "Ladies and gentlemen, the captain has just turned on the fasten seat belt sign." It can strike cold terror into your heart or matter-of-factly reassure you that the pilot is up there in the cockpit thinking of your safety and comfort in flight. It depends on the tone of voice, speed of delivery, and all kinds of subtleties I haven't the language to express, but you as a passenger will readily understand. Now think of stories you've heard patients tell about the discovery of a lump, arrhythmia, or abnormal Pap smear. What did the examining clinician's tone of voice convey? No question, the patient will be able to tell you. How was the patient told or not told about what the unexpected finding meant? How was her response heard or not heard? Were there setbacks resulting from ignorance, arrogance, or clumsiness? Or was healing enhanced by the calm, smooth course of the work-up and subsequent treatment.

In this era of high tech, speed, and the bottom line, it is easy to dismiss the healing art as the soft, ultimately dispensable side of medicine. It is common to assume its presence or forgive its absence in professional practice. But art is the power behind the placebo effect. It can disarm threats to health and trigger immune response. It can mitigate fear, pain, and suffering. Healing art heals.

Those duped by the rhetoric of the medical-industrial complex might think of the skilled professional as an interchangeable widget or jack of all trades. They will be proved wrong. True healers are masters of their art.

I realize that nobody ever taught me the art
of nursing. But along the way, a number of artists
showed me their palettes.

PHOTO: CONSTANCE PIERCE

Healing art

I'm trying to figure out how I learned the healing
art—what I know of it, that is. How did I learn about
the wisdom that surpasses knowledge? the facility
that lies beyond skill? How did I get a feel for the
intangibles that contribute to well-being? the elements of style that ignite a patient's healing potential? the aura of power and sense of possibility
that emanate from healers? How did I begin to
grasp these things?

Not in school and not from textbooks.
Wait, that isn't strictly true. There was a teacher.
It started with a teacher. Her last name was
Harter. Her first name was Miss. She was a nurse's
nurse, master of her art. A woman of a certain age, she was tall and
solidly built—or maybe that's just how I remember her. She glided
silently through hospital corridors like a clipper ship with a large,
square, white cap for a mainsail.

I can still recall oddments from her Surgical Specialties course in
the summer of 1962, but it's not the content that matters. It's not anything that happened in the classroom, although I worked as hard for
her approval there as I have ever worked for anybody's anywhere.
What impressed me and set so many aspirations vibrating in my head
was how things happened around her whenever she was on the wards.
In short, they fell into place. And I acquired a rudimentary under-

standing of hygiene and order, calm and comfort, responsibility and authority as if by osmosis while in her charge.

Since Miss Harter, there have been many others from whom I have learned the healing art. Very early in my career there was my high school classmate, Ruth. An RN at nineteen after completing a two-year degree program, I was acting head nurse on the unit where Ruth, a nursing student in a four-year program, was working for the summer as an aide. She had an irritating way of seeing the big picture, wanting to know what would happen to Mrs. Curry after she was discharged with the colostomy, for example, and how we could help Mr. Benson when he got so depressed after the wound infection. All I knew was there was no time to deal with any of this. My staff is straining just to make it though the shift and here is Baby Ruth asking unanswerable questions. But I watched her with patients and thought there must be things about nursing she grasped and I didn't—yet.

Then there was Aileen, a friend who was Director of Nursing at the hospital where I was doing private duty. Still in my novitiate, I came very nearly unhinged by the endless demands of my first celebrity patient. One afternoon in Aileen's office, I finally let my anxiety and frustration spill out. Next morning I watched as she swept into my patient's room like any other executive, dressed to impress, gracious, and very definitely In Charge. She sat on his bed—SAT ON HIS BED!!—and chatted with him about this and that in a blaze of savoir-faire that left me awestruck. Whatever had been wrong she made better with a sprinkling of some kind of fairy dust. How did she do that?

While working at the Visiting Nurse Association, I dropped in on two of my colleagues who shared a house. It was about 8:00 in the evening. There they were, on the floor, chatting about the day, their patients' records strewn around them like photos for an album. So, the care doesn't end when the patient's door shuts behind you. I was afraid of that.

Lucia from Hospice. I'd worked so hard to foster The Dynamic Nurse-Patient Relationship with this young diplomat, dying of cancer. And what did Lucia do to win him over for all time? She got his vein in one try. Every time. He could count on it. Nothing else mattered more.

Barbara at the clinic on Ninth Street. What was it in her voice that made that bawdy, balky ambulance crew lift that reeking, bleeding homeless man in our waiting room onto a stretcher and out into the evening for a run to the ER? She never shouted. Never threatened.

Tony in his office, Italian opera in the deep background, defining him in some way, personalizing and resonating with the healer-patient duet.

Rhonda and those ubiquitous roses—everywhere in the Well Woman Clinic from the stirrup covers to the letterhead. They were her logo, her promise. And that purple pin with "Listen to Women" in bold. I saw the women look at it, saw them getting the message.

Reflecting on my own experience, I realize that nobody ever taught me the art of nursing. But along the way, a number of artists showed me their palettes, let me hear them play their instruments, sample their recipes. And I simply took it all in like a hungry guest at a magnificent buffet.

ENTRY #49: **Thank-You Note**

I didn't receive many thank-you notes during my years at Community Medical Care, but here's one I treasure. Pat, one of the most hopelessly addicted alcoholics I'd ever nursed, taught me an important lesson.

Dear Veneta,

...I've been home [in England] for almost 4 years now and it's good to be back, tho I miss America of course. I had lived in Maryland and DC most of my life from the age of eighteen. I'm almost 52 years old now and wonder how those years went so quickly.

I often think about when you prayed for me because I was really going downhill with drinking. Drink doesn't bother me at all now, I don't even think about it. I might have an occasional one at Christmas or a celebration. I'm still hooked on those darn cigarettes tho, and they are very expensive in this country, as is just about everything. Still I get by and am thankful.

I still take medicine for my blood pressure and stomach tho, but I'm just fine and please God I hope to see you again when I visit DC. Soon I hope. Tell Sharon and Dr. Hall and everyone I say Hi. Take care, Veneta.

Love, Pat

Clinic volunteer, economist Vern Renshaw, believes that
the caring functions once ceded to health professionals
will revert to the family and community in the future
because they are too nebulous to define, measure,
and pay for. But I worry about a health care system
devoid of personality.

I was being introduced to the supervising physician at the large HMO
where I've been putting in some extra hours evenings and weekends.
"Oh, you'll do fine here," she said encouragingly. "We have a lot of
experience working with midlevels."

I smiled and continued the conversation without missing a beat, but
inside something went thud. Something to do with the prospect of working as a midlevel in a large organization—a sort of anonymous cog in
the powerful engine that seems to be driving the future of health care in
this country.

I've been a registered nurse for over thirty years and a nurse practitioner for fifteen of them. In my daytime job, I am one of three primary
health care providers in a small inner-city clinic that ekes out its income
from sliding-scale fees, Medicaid, Medicare, and contributions. I am
responsible for the ongoing care of a large number of children, adults,
and seniors who range from well to sick, stable to labile, easy to complicated. It's been a long time since I've considered myself at midlevel in
my nursing career.

And now here I am, a part-time staffer in the after-hours program
of a prepaid medical plan serving mostly middle-class suburbanites with
a different set of expectations and demands from those I have become
accustomed to. Most likely I will see "my patients" only once, for
the can't-wait problem that brought them in, then refer them on to their

regular provider. It's a good system and it pays me well—over three times what I earn at Community Medical Care. There is an easy collegiality among staff members. I can get consultation on the spot whenever I need it. And I don't have to worry about how to wangle diagnostic studies, medications, or appointments with specialists for patients with no money or insurance plans. It's all available right on the premises, prepaid.

My greatest challenge is to use my knowledge and experience to transcend the cost-effective midlevel provider role mapped out for me and to do this in a setting where brisk efficiency is valued. I want my one-time patients to leave the medical center feeling better for having been in my care, even if the encounter lasted no more than ten minutes. For example, I make a point of sitting down when I enter the room. Sure, it takes a load off my feet, but I hope it also gives the impression that I am settling in and preparing to pay attention. I listen as long as possible before interrupting—even when I'm convinced I can guess the rest of the relevant history. I try to be therapeutic in my use of touch and to teach some basics about the course of the illness. On principle, I always include information about non-drug treatment options even when I know the whole purpose of my patient's trek out into the night has been to get an antibiotic prescription. I try to sympathize when she tells me accusingly that she can't afford to be sick—as if I might be in possession of a cure I am churlishly withholding.

> I want my one-time patients to leave the medical center feeling better for having been in my care, even if the encounter lasted no more than ten minutes.

I notice, too, that I usually enlarge my focus beyond the immediate problem to take a look at the big picture. How is this illness affecting daily life? What stressors may have contributed to the patient's getting sick in the first place? It takes time, but I claim it as my professional prerogative. And, despite the fact that care is presumably continuing outside my realm, I have made occasional follow-up telephone calls as much for my benefit as the patient's — a habit I adopted from another after-hours nurse practitioner.

My friend Vern, an economist and health care reform watcher, believes that the caring-nursing functions once ceded to health professionals will revert to the family or community in the future. They are simply too nebulous to define, measure, and pay for in our financially strapped, high-tech, problem-oriented medical culture.

But I worry about a health care system devoid of personality. In my experience, the healer has always been at least as important as the tools he or she uses to effect healing. Even a standard protocol plays out differently depending on who is following it. For me — a savvy, well-insured health professional — and for my patients at Community Medical Care — a motley group of mostly poor, uninsured and unsophisticated health care "consumers" who may one day be handed a Health Security card — I want to preserve choice: choice of providers, health care settings, and levels of technology. Despite the body of science on which the practice of medicine and nursing is based, we all know there is no one right way to cure anything. I trust people to know what and who makes them feel better. Wherever I work — and whatever my title — I want to remember who I am and what I have to offer. Lord knows, the future needs nursing.

Perhaps the rise of technology does not presage the death of caregiving. At least one futurist speculates that in the postmodern era those who perform the "complex and difficult" caring tasks will hold high-status jobs.

Everyone tackles journal reading in their own way. Some go directly to the table of contents to scan for pertinent topics. Others page through casually, front to back, or back to front, looking for a title, abstract, or picture to pique their curiosity. Then there are those who have favorite sections and head straight for them—the back page with the human interest story, the want ads, the news capsules, the clinical pearls column.

With me, no matter what the journal, it's the editorials and letters to the editor I flip to first. I want to know what's on the editor's mind and what issues he or she wants me to think about. Then I want to know what, in fact, other readers are thinking—how they have responded to previous articles, what has gotten them fired up enough to write public letters to their peers. Most of all, I like controversy. An author claims, a reader begs to differ, the author replies, another reader weighs in, and so on.

Several months ago, there was an editorial on the art and aesthetics of nursing scholarship that caught my eye. I wasn't exactly certain what this meant but was reassured when the editor quoted an authority who said, "It takes both art and science to truly connect people and make us all whole."[21] My sentiments exactly. That's why I'm a nurse and a poet and why I believe the practice of the one feeds the other. I ripped out the editorial page and put it in my "good ideas" file.

When the following issue of the journal arrived, I opened to the letters. Ah, controversy! Under the subhead "A decent paying job—not art and beauty," there was a letter from a reader in distress. A nurse practitioner, like me. An NP battling the establishment over third-party reimbursement, like me. But wait, not like me. She wrote: "I am not interested in the art and beauty of nursing! … [W]hile I worry about whether I will be employed a year from now… I do not need to consider the aesthetics of my practice. I need research that defends my existence!"[22]

My first reaction was to want to defend *my* existence—not as a nurse, but as a poet. And that is what I did in my own letter to the editor (another reader weighs in). We already have such research, and it has not bought us a place at the table, I wrote. Ultimately, decisions about our future will be political and irrational and will reflect our position in the popular culture. Norman Rockwell could do us more good than the *New England Journal of Medicine.* So could cartoon strips like *Doonesbury* and television shows like "ER" (I decided not to risk mentioning poets, even Walt Whitman).

Only later did I tune in to the feelings of impending doom that seem to permeate not just that letter, but much of our recent professional literature. We must be "as good as" or "better than" or even "unique" in order to survive. Why? Granted, the future of professions as we know them is indeed open to speculation, as is the future of paid work. But I happen to hold with the futurist Jeremy Rifkin who writes that, "While market-oriented tasks—even highly technical and professional jobs—are often reducible to digitization and computerization, caring tasks that require intimate relationships between people are far too complex and difficult to be attended to by high-tech software. In the postmodern era, these are high-status jobs."[23]

Nursing will continue to evolve as an essential and respected activity in the information age. This is a given. A robot can perform a hip replacement, but it can't nurse the patient back to health. A computer software program can spit out the differential diagnosis, work-up, plan of treatment, and likelihood of cure for a child's condition, but it can't nurse the anxious parents and the child in the throes of the illness.

So let's celebrate the art of nursing through art. And for me, that includes work songs, protest songs, poster art, artfully designed and decorated work spaces, inspirational verse, stories from our professional experience, formal debate, stand-up comedy—the gamut of personal expression. A decent paying job, yes, *and* art and beauty.

Note card featuring a drawing by second-grader Brittani Crouch (see page 205)

The Crisis of Health Care as a Crisis of Wisdom

In this excerpt from the annual report, Jim, a physician whose mission extends to the healing of the earth, presented his response to the national debate on health care reform.

We often think that we live in the information age, but perhaps the opposite is closer to the truth. Bill McKibben suggests that we live in an "Age of Missing Information." In a book by that name, McKibben contrasted the information imparted on two very different "days" in his life. One "day" consisted of all the programming on cable TV in Fairfax, Virginia, in one twenty-four-hour day (over a thousand hours) which he arranged to have videotaped and subsequently reviewed. Interspersed with excerpts of this information are accounts from the other "day" which was spent camping and hiking on a mountain in the Adirondacks in New York. He discovered that what was missing from the modern world was "information about the physical limits of a finite world, about sufficiency and need, about proper scale and real time, about the sensual pleasure of exertion and exposure to the elements, about the need for community and for solid, real skills."

Like Bill McKibben, I have been to the mountain. I spent two days in August camping on a bluff overlooking the small cove where the Goose River flows into the Bay of Fundy. I hiked to the spring and back to bring water for breakfast. I crossed the cove at low tide and climbed the bluffs on the other side, returning before the onrushing tide made return impossible. I cooked dinner under a hastily erected shelter as the rain began to fall in earnest. I have discovered for myself some of the missing information— information about limits, about sufficiency, about exposure to the elements, and the need for solid, real skills. I have touched another world of "information"—the deep mystery of God at the heart of creation.

I am aware of the contrast between the wisdom of the mountain and the modern, "information age" practice of medicine...

PHOTO: JIM HALL

But wisdom has yet to show up in the national debate on health care reform. What has shown up, at least on those TV channels in Fairfax, Virginia, in the "information age," is a great deal of unintelligible language, inflammatory rhetoric, and a wholesale shift in focus from the future of health care to the future of the Clinton presidency. What confirmation that ours is an age of missing information, of lost wisdom!

I propose that we take the future of our health care system and place it in the hands of those in whom wisdom still resides — the hands of wounded healers, of shamans, the hands of grandmothers and grandfathers, especially. I would place it in the hands of those who have suffered the long road with illness and found healing and caring and community along the way. I would put it in the hands of those who have walked a long time on ocean beaches and written poems and of those who have walked the mountain ridges and watched the hawks fly south. I would, in short, entrust it to those who have learned the physical limits of a finite world, to those who know about sufficiency and need, about proper scale and real time, and to those who know the need for community and for solid, real skills. And, most certainly, to those who have touched the deep mystery of God at the heart of all things.

In 1978 when Community Medical Care opened its doors on Ninth Street, we wanted to make available a small, personal, direct form of primary care, a combination of nurse and doctor, of curing and caring, to a part of the city where there were few "private doctors." Since then, many have found us here, but no one has followed us. Now, fewer and fewer doctors are setting up "private" practices anywhere, and nurse/ doctor collaborative practices are an endangered species.

The house that is our health care system is being torn down and rebuilt. What sort of a house do we want to have? What do we need less of for it to be more whole? What do we need more of that healing may happen? Who will teach us and show us the way?

When CMC opened its doors in 1978, I would never have imagined that my tenure there would last seventeen years. But as the time to leave grew nearer, I could not imagine my life without it. This was my last contribution to the annual report, the traditional "Dear Friends" letter that greeted clinic supporters on the first page and summarized events of the past year.

DECEMBER 1994

"Who's going to do the Dear Friends letter this year?" I asked Sharon the other day as plans for this year's annual report lurched along. It was either her or me since everyone else planning to contribute had already staked out their territory. Before she could think more about it, I popped the question. "Can I do it?" I asked.

I suddenly realized that I wanted very much to write this letter. Not only because it's been ten years since I last had the honor. Not only because, through years of correspondence — telling you how things are with us, asking for your support, thanking you for it — I've come to think of you as family. Not only because we've weathered a year of struggle as DC Medicaid, our major source of third-party payments, launched its managed care program in a whirlwind of confusion, causing a crisis of lost income and shaking our confidence in the future. I really wanted to write this letter because 1995 will likely be my last year as nurse and director at Community Medical Care.

With a certainty that I cannot explain, and even regret, I know that it is time for me to leave CMC and prepare myself to embark on the next step of my journey. Why? I ask myself. I've always said that no matter what lies ahead, I'll always look back on this as the best job I ever

PHOTO: JIM HALL

Our thank-you note to contributors

had. This is where I've learned to understand nursing as healing through care and nurture, and where I've learned that, when it comes to providing health care for people who are poor or on the margin, small is beautiful and personality is essential. CMC really is like the mom-and-pop stores that dot our neighborhood. We're small, located in a residential area, and offer a familiar array of "the main things." We've been around a generation or so and we're personal—we'll remember anyone who comes a couple times and probably already know some of the same people they know. And, of course, we give credit.

As I know you already know, at CMC we do a lot with a little. When we use that expression, we're usually talking about money. But CMC has also done a lot with my life. It has been a source of inspiration for poetry and essays on health care. It has been a primary source of friendship and of professional, personal, and spiritual growth. It has brought out the best and the worst in me. It has been a place where healing happens. Even more important, it has been some of these things for a great many of our patients.

This year we depend on your support every bit as much as we always have. As an organization we, like our patients, are on the margin. With a bank balance that has seldom amounted to more than a month's expenses, any change in the political, bureaucratic, or our own corporate climate could knock us out of commission. We need your contributions and your prayers.

In return, we send you our thanks and blessings for the new year. And if you ever find yourself poor, sick, and uninsured, we'll welcome you with open arms.

Although I can't point to it as a model to be replicated, Community Medical Care has been, for me, an idyllic place in which to practice nursing. As I prepare to leave, I wonder whether the fruits of my experience at the clinic will continue to nourish me as I labor in the next vineyard.

I don't know how else to put it. Leaving Community Medical Care, the little inner-city mom-and-pop clinic where I've worked for almost seventeen years, feels exactly like leaving home. "So why do it?" friends ask. "Because it's time," I say.

Not that it will be easy. There are my colleagues who are like family — *are* family. Sure we've had our squabbles, our creative tensions, 0but we've been through a lot together as low-budget, people-oriented caregivers within a system that values high-tech, procedure-oriented "cures." How will I manage without them?

Then there are my patients. I've come to know most of them not just as individuals but as families, extended families, buildings full of families. Saying goodbye is painful, even to the ones who, as my patient Ernest Williams likes to say, "look better goin' than comin'." I know I am leaving them in good hands, but there have always been those who were in my bag, who felt more like "mine" than "ours." I will miss them.

A deeper understanding of the nature of nursing and medicine is part of the bountiful harvest my work at the clinic has yielded: nursing as healing through care and nurture; medicine as the diagnosis and treatment of disease; the two poles at the extremes of a continuum along which doctors and nurses move in response to the demands and constraints of their practice and their own gravitational pull.

My gleanings don't stop there. I've gained a sense of the importance of personality to healing; the importance of ambiance, of faith, magic, drama, potions; the importance of keeping it small, keeping it simple if you want to connect with people on the fringes of society; and the importance of being there, day to day, year to year, if you want to win their trust. I've acquired a profound respect for the power of money—to keep the doors open, to support one's family, and to bolster one's self-respect, yes—but also as a means to express cultural values (cultural values being what health care reform is all about). Will these fruits of my experience at Community Medical Care continue to nourish me as I labor in the next vineyard?

I am aware that, while moving on is a challenge I have set for myself voluntarily, it is one many nurses are facing involuntarily. Hospital units close—entire hospitals close. Nurses lose their jobs or are stretched to the limit as available funds diminish or are diverted. Advanced practice nurses take house staff roles. Staff nurses are forced to practice McNursing—purveying services from a limited menu, fast, no substitutions. Nurses move outside the walls to the community where they find the patients they discharged early still in need of acute care at home. Traditional home care nurses find their long-term, chronically ill patients dropped from the agency rolls because the services they need are not covered by insurance. They will likely end up back in the hospital or in nursing homes, which are also expensive. Public health nurses are squeezed into narrow, tightly-focused programs funded with soft money for as long as their goals (fight AIDS, reduce rates of teenage pregnancy, whatever) remain in vogue. Meanwhile, nurses in primary health care find themselves working as physician extenders because time-intensive nursing care costs too much and, well, takes too much time.

Making sick neighborhoods healthy requires more than health care. Rare and fragile are organizations like Community Medical Care which exercise the right to flout convention by forfeiting the security of a living wage and standard working conditions for staff. What, for me, has been an idyllic place in which to practice nursing, is nothing I can point to as a model to be replicated — nothing our society seems willing to pay for on a large scale. Nor can I boast that CMC has turned a sick neighborhood into a healthy one. That would require a lot more than just health care.

What I think of as leaving home, someone else might call progress. We all have to move on, keep up with the times, change, push the envelope. That's the American way. And, although we Americans like to tout our ideals, we are famous for our mastery of the art of the possible. The fact is, I don't like what I see in the mainstream of modern health care, but there's not much sense in blinding myself to it. The most I can reasonably do is keep a healthy distance — that, and find a new niche on the margin where I can nurse the possible into being.

This is the brief note I wrote in my journal on
June 2, 1995, my last day at Community Medical Care.

It was a typical primary health care encounter in every respect except
one: it was my last at Community Medical Care. The patient was Olivia,
a Salvadoran woman I knew slightly. She said she had a headache and
her nerves were bothering her. There was no emotional farewell at the
end—we didn't know each other well enough for that. I simply told her
that, next time, she would be seeing Jim, Teresa, or our new nurse
practitioner, Quincy, because this was my last day. Soon after, I slipped
out the back door. I couldn't face another goodbye. This evening at
the farewell party, I sat with a paper crown on my head. Kevin [Sharon's
son and my godson—a child of six whom I had seen almost every
day of his life from the time he was first installed in a basket under the
front desk where his mother worked] came over to ask me if it was my
birthday. "No," I said. "We're having a party because I'm leaving the
clinic."

"Oh," he said. "Well,
drive safely."

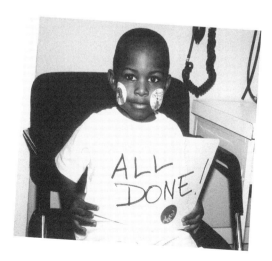

Epilogue

Five years have passed since I left Community Medical Care, but whenever I refer to the clinic, I still say "we." As if I had never said goodbye.

That's not to say that the little clinic on Ninth Street, now in its twenty-second year, is the same as when I left it. As folks in the neighborhood would say, "Mmm, mmph. It is surely goin' through some changes." The most obvious is the cavernous pit right across the street that opened up and swallowed six city blocks, just like that. Out of this gaping hole, crawling with men and machines, a new DC convention center is expected to rise sometime within the next five years. The construction has literally shaken CMC's foundations. Ninth Street is closed. Pedestrian access to the small businesses still open on the block is restricted to a narrow wooden walkway.

That's outside. Inside the clinic, the bureaucratic exigencies of managed care have also shaken things up. For example, staff no longer decide what lab to affiliate with and where to refer patients who need specialty care. And, for Medicaid patients, payment is no longer by fee for service but by capitation—a fixed amount for each person who designates CMC as their primary source of care. The computerization of billing and bookkeeping, which took so many years to complete, may have streamlined some operations but it has also made them more complex. Not surprisingly, the number of support and administrative staff (but not the number of income-generating "providers") has increased. Given the big chunk of the budget now earmarked for overhead, clinic finances are even more uncertain than they were in "my day."

And, for the first time—perhaps as a result of the times—the staff has entered a phase of instability. Sharon, who succeeded me as director, and Quincy, who took my place as nurse practitioner, have both moved on to the next chapter of their lives. Even "Pop" himself, Jim Hall, is poised to leave the clinic and embark on a new career in restoration ecology, a formalization of his long-term commitment to the healing of the land.

Urla, the clinic's third director since my departure, recently completed a "definitely challenging and at times overwhelming" first year. Could she, I wonder, imagine handling the administration "in the cracks" between clinic sessions as Jim and I once did? But her vision for CMC is larger than ours ever was and includes a new, spacious building, street outreach, a nutrition program, prenatal care (once again) and mental health services. She also wants to diversify the clinic's funding base and secure federal funds for the first time.

No doubt about it, CMC is moving through the kind of life cycle typical of small organizations that must change with the times to survive. Teresa, who will soon be the senior clinician on staff, is worried that in all the hullabaloo over money, a new place, and staff changes, it will be all too easy to lose sight of the clinic's primary mission: healing people, one at a time, in a way that is both highly professional and warmly personal. "Soup and Stories" was her inspiration. She conceived it as a time for the staff to gather around a deep pot of hearty soup and share the stories of their life together. A way to nourish both body and soul. She even invited me to come and reminisce about "the old days."

I accepted with pleasure. For three years after leaving CMC, I had worked in the Well Woman Clinic at a nearby army base and, to my surprise, loved it. But then I took an even more radical step. After thirty-five years as a nurse, I decided to grant myself a sabbatical and a rest from the intensity of direct patient care. During that year, I wrote some and explored some and gradually felt my way toward the path I'm on today: practicing the art of healing through writing and caring for caregivers. I fear for the future of professional caregiving in this country. I am afraid that it will be done in by the careless and expensive demands of a soulless brand of medical techno-wizardry that seems heedless of the cost in human suffering. I want to help by taking good care of those who will one day, I hope, be there to take care of you and me.

It was on this mission that I arrived for Soup and Stories on a Friday at noon. As we sat in the upstairs room we call "the chapel," soup bowls warming our laps, I started by retelling a story I'd just read by Barry Lopez called "Winter Count 1973." The winter count is a traditional way of marking time among some Native American tribes. All through the slow winter months, the elders ponder the events of the year past, then decide on one that most clearly captures the essence of that year. One elder's choice may differ from another's. As Lopez writes, "…it is too dangerous for everyone to have the same story. The same things do not happen to everyone." But, in the aggregate, these stories add to the collective memory that binds a people together. For instance, mention the Saturday old Margaret fell asleep on the downstairs toilet in an alcoholic stupor and could not be roused, causing chaos in the operations of the clinic, and not only that event, but a whole era, springs vividly back to mind.

I told a tale or two of mine and then read a few excerpts from my treasured collection of CMC's annual reports. Soon enough, the others were telling their stories. Like the one about Wilma's conversion from tough-talking addict in the streets to almost demure West Virginia country gal. Who'd have imagined it? And she's still healthy *and* HIV positive after all these years! The result, entirely predictable, was hilarity and a few moist eyes. The soup was delicious. By the time we had to call it quits and open the doors for afternoon office hours, I think it's fair to say that the hunger of all present had been, in some fundamental way, satisfied.

"The same things do not happen to everyone." As I reread this notebook, I see how personal it is. What I've written is not what Jim or Teresa or Sharon—or any other nurse in the city—would write. But, speaking now as an elder, I hope it becomes part of the winter count of the Tribe of Caregivers, that is to say, part of the lore and the communal vision that hold us together and move us forward.

My thanks to the editors of the following journals in which these essays first appeared:

American Journal of Nursing

Undercover Nursing, February 1992

In My Prime, April 1992

Are We Ready to Answer? [A Ready Answer], June 1992

Mindset, August 1992

Seven Keys to Nursing, October 1992

$5 Day, December 1992

Prescriptive Ambivalence, February 1993

My Life as a Symptom, April 1993

The More-with-Less Notebook June 1993

Journal of Christian Nursing

When Sugarplums Go Sour, Summer 1994

Nursing and Health Care Perspectives

Scouting My Future, April 1994

Leaving Home, June 1995

Health Care as Performance Art, Mar/Apr 1996

A Decent Paying Job—Not Art and Beauty, May/Jun 1996

Skill, Jul/Aug 1996

Healers' Apprentice, Sep/Oct 1996

Nursing Outlook

Nurses and Doctors as Healers, Mar/Apr 1985

A Case for Doctoring Nursing, May/Jun 1988

If New Graduates Went to the Community First, Jul/Aug 1988

Facing AIDS, Sep/Oct 1988

Slicing the Salary Pie, Nov/Dec 1988

Upstairs, Downstairs, Jan/Feb 1989
Pushing the Outside of the Envelope, Mar/Apr 1989
Health for All at Ninth & P, May/Jun 1989
Clinical Scholarship and the Pragmatic Practitioner, Jul/Aug 1989
A Room of One's Own, Nov/Dec 1989
A Good Nurse, Jan/Feb 1990
Political Subversion on Ninth & P? [Nurse in Neighborhood Clinic
    Disappeared], Mar/Apr 1990
A Place to Heal, May/Jun 1990
Nursing the Charts, Jul/Aug 1990
What This City Needs is More Mom-and-Pops, Sep/Oct 1990
Tools of the Trade, Jan/Feb 1991
Bring Back Big Nurse, Mar/Apr 1991
Asking the Question, May/Jun 1991
The Art of the Matter, Jul/Aug 1991
On Pregnancy Tests, Sep/Oct 1991

World Health
    Primary Health Care in Washington, DC, July 1982

The poem "Witness" was published both in *Faith@Work* (Spring 1999)
and in the anthology *The Arduous Touch—Women's Voices in Health Care*,
edited by Amy Marie Haddad and Kate H. Brown (Purdue University
Press, 1999). "Maggie Jones," originally written for the 1985 annual
report of Community Medical Care, was subsequently published in the
Journal of Christian Nursing (Summer 1987). Both "Maggie Jones" and
"Another Case of Chronic Pelvic Pain," written for the 1991 annual
report, appear in *Rehab at the Florida Avenue Grill* (Sage Femme Press, 1999).

I also want to express my profound gratitude to
Jim Hall, Teresa Acquaviva, and Sharon Baskerville, for the use of some of their contributions to the annual reports of Community Medical Care — and for so much more

Lucie Kelly, who took a chance on "Microcosmos," and Edith "Pat" Lewis, astute editor, faithful correspondent, wry sage

Doris Bloch, Lisa Carey, and Nancy Evans for wise counsel, creative support, and editorial acumen

New Community Church and the larger Church of the Saviour faith community in which my vocation continues to be forged and blessed

My husband Frank, whose partnership through 25 years has enabled me to follow my heart

For your information
What Do Nurses Do? by Melodie Chenevert, RN is a coloring book published by Pro-Nurse Press, 15 Park Avenue, Gaithersburg MD 20877 (www.pronurse.com).

The two note cards shown in this book were produced by Window on Nursing, PO Box 1253, Olney MD 20830 (www.windowonnursing.com)

1. *Nursing: A Social Policy Statement* (Kansas City, MO: American Nurses' Association, 1980), Publ. No. NP-63.

2. I. C. Castillejo, *Knowing Woman: A Feminine Psychology* (New York: Harper & Row, 1974), p. 15.

3. P. Benner, "From Novice to Expert," *American Journal of Nursing* 82:402-407, March 1982.

4. Castillejo, p. 103.

5. R. Wartzman, "AIDS Heaps Hardship on Washington Slum Called 'The Graveyard,'" *Wall Street Journal*, 4 November 1987.

6. T. Wolfe, *The Right Stuff* (New York: Bantam Books, 1984) pp.8–9.

7. M. E. Rogers, "Nursing is coming of age...through the practitioner movement: Con," *American Journal of Nursing* 75:1834–1843, October 1975.

8. *Alma Ata 1978 — Primary Health Care*, Geneva: World Health Organization, 1978.

9. D. Diers, "On Clinical Scholarship (Again)," *Image: The Journal of Nursing Scholarship* 20:2, Spring 1988.

10. V. Woolf, *A Room of One's Own* (New York: Harcourt Brace Jovanovich, 1929).

11. Castillejo, op. cit.

12. T. Lewin, "Sudden Nurse Shortage Threatens Hospital Care," *New York Times*, 7 July 1987.

13. P. J. Maraldo and S. B. Solomon, "Nursing's Window of Opportunity," *Image: The Journal of Nursing Scholarship* 19:83–86, Summer 1987.

14. P. Moccia, "The Nature of the Nursing Shortage: Will Crisis Become Structure?" *Nursing and Health Care* 8:321–322, June 1987.

15. M. F. Fralic, "Again So Soon? Thoughts On the Nurse Shortage," *Nursing and Health Care* 8:209–210, April 1987.

16. F. Nightingale, *Notes on Nursing* (New York: Dover Publications, 1969), p. 9.

17. J. C. Hays, "Voices in the Record," *Image: The Journal of Nursing Scholarship* 21:200–204, Winter 1989.

18. K. Kesey, *One Flew Over the Cuckoo's Nest* (New York: Viking Press, 1962).

19. D. Hall, *Contemporary American Poetry*, (Baltimore, MD: Penguin Books, 1962), p. 29.

20. C. Sims, "Dinkins Announces Health-Care Plan to Serve the Poor," *New York Times*, 21 April 1992.

21. B. Henry, "Art, Aesthetics, Science, Nursing," *Image: The Journal of Nursing Scholarship* 27:2, First Quarter, 1995.

22. N. W. O'Rourke, "A Decent Paying Job — Not Art and Beauty," *Image: The Journal of Nursing Scholarship* 27: 90, Second Quarter, 1995.

23. J. Rifkin, "Choosing Our Future," *Utne Reader*, May-June 1995, p. 57.

Veneta Masson is a nurse, poet, and essayist living in Washington, DC.
A 1963 graduate of the Associate Degree Nursing Program at Pasadena
City College in California, she also holds a B.S. in nursing from the
University of California, San Francisco, an M.A. from the University
of Washington, and post-Master's certification as a family nurse
practitioner from the University of Virginia. In 1991, she was named
Nurse of the Year by the District of Columbia Nurses Association.
The University of Washington School of Nursing selected her as
Distinguished Alumna in 1998.

Her most recent book of poetry, *Rehab at the Florida Avenue Grill*
(Sage Femme Press), complements this one with poems from
her thirty-five years in nursing, in particular the seventeen years at
Community Medical Care.

PHOTO: ROBERT GIARD